MEN AND WOMEN OF THE
NEW TESTAMENT

MEN AND WOMEN OF THE
NEW TESTAMENT

DEREK THOMAS

AUTUMN

HOUSE

British Library Cataloguing in Publishing
Data. A catalogue record for this book
is available from the British Library.

All scripture quotations are from the New
International Version unless stated otherwise.

ISBN 1-873796-72-2

Published by
Autumn House
Alma Park, Grantham, Lincolnshire,
NG31 9SL, England.

ABOUT THE AUTHOR

William Derek Thomas served for thirty years as a Baptist minister. At present he is combining pastoral work with research at the University of Lancaster.

Revd Thomas was born in Merthyr Tydfil, becoming a committed Christian at 17. On leaving school he trained as an engineer until he felt God's call to ministry. His ministerial training took place at the Bristol Baptist College, and his theological education at the Universities of Bristol and London.

After ordination to the Baptist ministry Revd Thomas served in Merthyr, Swansea, Wrexham and the Scarisbrick New Road Baptist church, Southport. He is married to Gwyneth, a nursing sister, and they have four children and eight grandchildren.

He has made frequent, and well received, contributions to the *Expository Times*. His hobbies include sport, music and travel. His current research project centres around the attutude of Jesus towards women.

MEN AND WOMEN OF THE
NEW TESTAMENT

W. DEREK THOMAS

The Christian faith has a many-sided appeal. Some are drawn to faith by its profound teachings; others by the faithful witness of the Church across the centuries. One of the most interesting sidelights of our understanding and appreciation of the Christian movement is the way it is seen in the lives of the men and women whose names we meet in the New Testament pages. What a kaleidoscope of varied experiences and fortunes they represent!

These men and women are our ancestors in the faith, and though — with one glorious exception — they are dead, their lives, loves, and loyalties, including, too, their weaknesses, and recovery, speak to us today.

W. Derek Thomas has done well to assemble a set of some thirty thumb-nail sketches of these folk. Expressed in an easy-to-read collection of chapters, their careers are retold, and their lessons applied. They live again as his pen deftly portrays their example and warning.

I recommend heartily these pages to any prospective readers especially preachers and teachers. But all will learn something, and be encouraged.

RALPH P. MARTIN
Fuller Theological Seminary
School of Theology, Pasadena, California

CONTENTS

JESUS
'The hope of every contrite heart'
MATTHEW 1:21

When Napoleon had time to reflect during the enforced seclusion of his exile, he thought a great deal about the life and significance of Jesus Christ. As a result of much musing, he wrote, 'Everything in Christ astonishes me. His Spirit overawes me, His will confounds me. Between Him and whoever else in the world there is no possible term of comparison.' Carnegie Simpson expressed the same thought. 'Instinctively,' he wrote, 'we do not class Him with others. When one reads His name in a list beginning with Confucius and ending with Goethe we feel it is an offence less against orthodoxy than decency. Jesus is not one of the group of the world's greatest. Talk about Alexander the Great and Napoleon the Great if you will . . . Jesus is apart. He is not the 'great'. He is the only. He is simply Jesus . . . . He is beyond our analyses.'

Given that Jesus Christ is unique we may feel that the inclusion of a chapter about Him in a book about New Testament characters is tactlessly inept. He is not simply a character in the New Testament; He is the reason for the New Testament. And yet there is a sense in which the men and women we meet in its pages are really 'Jesus people'; their faith, their spiritual rebirth and growth, and their remarkable missionary exploits all flow from their union with Christ. Some account of the Person who made such a profound difference to them, therefore, is needed.

The two fundamental questions we can ask about Jesus may be expressed in the two interrogatives, 'Who' and 'What'. 'Who was Jesus?' and 'What did He do?' Many books have been written attempting to answer these questions, and anything that is said in this chapter will not be a complete or adequate account of the One whose Person is wrapped in mystery.

WHO IS JESUS?

There are times when the picture we have of Jesus in the gospels is of a truly human person, but then there are times when He shows Himself to be more than human. In fact, these two dimensions in the person of Jesus are interwoven sometimes in the same story. For example, in the account of the stilling of the storm on Galilee, Jesus is so tired after a hard and long day that He sleeps through a storm whose ferocity unnerves experienced seagoing fishermen. Here is human fatigue. Yet the same Jesus stands up, addresses the elements and controls the forces of nature. The disciples were dumbfounded at His authority.

In the story of the raising of Lazarus, Jesus wept (John 11:35). The tears were probably shed not so much because of the death of Lazarus — since, according to John, Jesus knew that Lazarus would be raised — but because of the distress Jesus felt when he saw the anguish of Mary and Martha in their bereavement. That is the point in the story when He weeps and not when He first heard the news of the death of Lazarus. It was a very human reaction. Yet the same Jesus raised Lazarus from the dead, and many who witnessed this miracle believed in Him (John 11:45).

The great creeds of the Church reflect this human/divine way of understanding Jesus. Where any theory has stressed one aspect of the human/divine nature of Jesus to the negating of the other, this has invariably been regarded as heresy. We now take a closer look at the two aspects of the Person of Christ.

☐ *He was truly human.* Jesus was neither a bionic man nor a superman; He did not live out His life by the continuous exercise of supernatural powers. Mainstream Christian thinkers have always rejected the idea that Jesus appeared merely in the *guise* of a human being, assuming a kind of phantom humanity. Eddie Askew has written: 'Salvation is gritty. It wasn't achieved by an ethereal spirit walking through the world six inches above the ground to keep his white robes

10

clean. Christ's feet trod where ours tread; in the dust, down where we are. He lived in the noise, tension and dirt of the world.'

Henry Parry Liddon made the point, 'If Jesus was not truly Man, the chasm between heaven and earth has not been bridged, and God — as before the Incarnation — is still remote and inaccessible.' The writer to the Hebrews makes a similar point as he stresses the true humanity of Jesus. He says that it was essential for Jesus to be made like His brothers in every way, 'so that he might be merciful and faithful as their high priest before God' (Heb. 2:17, NEB). By using the brother simile he is emphasizing Jesus' solidarity with the human family.

A poet writes,

> 'O Saviour Christ, Thou too art man;
> Thou hast been troubled, tempted, tried;
> Thy kind but searching glance can scan
> the very wounds that shame would hide.'

In this stanza, Henry Twells understands Christ as having entered fully into our human experience, that He has been where we are and has first-hand knowledge of us. He knows the whole truth about us and can 'scan the very wounds that shame would hide', yet His purpose is to heal.

□ *He was divine.* In claiming that Jesus was the Son of God in a Trinitarian sense, we are unquestionably embracing a mystery. To say that Jesus Christ is God is an affirmation whose full meaning is beyond our power to comprehend. Paul acknowledges this in his letter to Timothy when he wrote, 'Great is the mystery of godliness: he (some ancient manuscripts have 'God') was manifest in the flesh.' (1 Tim. 3:16, KJV.) Now since it is a great mystery what are the reasons that have convinced Christians that Christ was so closely identified with God that they felt justified in describing Him not only as the 'Son of God' but also as 'God the Son'? Of many such reasons we may note the following:

1. Many of the titles and prerogatives which belong

uniquely to God in the Old Testament are attributed, without qualification, to Jesus Christ in the New Testament. In the Old Testament, for example, God was usually spoken of as the 'Lord' (Ps. 100:3). In the New Testament, the disciples regularly refer to Jesus as 'Lord' (John 6:68). The best-known Psalm speaks of God as the 'Shepherd' (Ps. 23), and in the New Testament Jesus speaks of Himself as 'the Good Shepherd' who knows His sheep and lays down His life for them (John 10:14, 15). God is described by Isaiah as the 'Redeemer' (Isa. 43:14) and in the New Testament Jesus accomplishes the work of redemption (Gal. 3:13; Rev. 5:9, KJV). In the book of Deuteronomy God is referred to as the 'Eternal' (Deut. 33:27). Jesus is characterized as the 'King eternal' (1 Tim. 4:17). In the Old Testament God is described as 'The first and the last' (Isa. 44:6) and in Revelation Jesus is portrayed in exactly the same way (Rev. 1:17, 18). As P. T. Forsyth wrote, 'He was the Son with a prologue of eternal history and an epilogue of the same.'

2. In the Bible worship is to be offered only to God. The people of God in the Old Testament were strictly forbidden to worship other gods (Exod. 34:14). And in this regard the New Testament is no different. In the Apocalypse, John is prohibited from worshipping an angel (Rev. 19:10) who remonstrates with him, '"Do not do it! I am a fellow-servant with you. . . . Worship God."' In the same vein, Paul and Barnabas reacted with shock and dismay when they heard that the people of Lystra were about to offer sacrifices to them, regarding the apostles as incarnations of the gods Zeus and Hermes. '"Men, why are you doing this?"' asks Paul. '"We are human beings just like you."' (Acts 14:15.)

This assiduous refusal by men and angels to assume the divine prerogative to be worshipped contrasts with the way Jesus accepts ascriptions of praise. When He entered Jerusalem and the crowds sang their Hosannas, some bystanders asked Him to restrain the disciples, perhaps sensing that their jubilant acclamations sounded like worship. Yet Jesus rejected that advice and accepted the adulation of the crowds, and did not think it inappropriate. In John's vision the Lamb (Jesus) receives worship from an unnumbered company of 'living creatures', 'elders' and 'many angels' who proclaim, '"Worthy is the Lamb who was slain, to receive power and wealth, wisdom and might, honour and glory and praise!"' (Rev. 5:12, REB.)

3. When Jesus pronounced forgiveness of sins to a paraplegic, some scribes resented what they believed to be a usurping of the prerogative of God. '"This is blasphemy!"' they said. '"Who but God alone can forgive sins?"' (Mark 1:7b, NEB.) Yet Jesus did not retract or apologize to them. Instead, He healed the man and thus further demonstrated His authority.

4. The most sacred thing for Jews was the law. The veneration with which the sacred scrolls are treated in the Jewish Synagogue today reminds us that the law was given by God to Moses and must be hallowed and obeyed. Only a person with divine status could restate the law as Jesus did. For instance, when the Pharisees spotted that Jesus' attitude to divorce was more rigorous than the lenient legislation laid down by Moses (Matt. 19:3-9), Jesus did not hesitate to point out that Moses permitted divorce as a concession to the 'stubbornness' of the people, but divorce was never God's intention. Moses' pragmatic response to the needs of fallible human beings might have been justified, but God's purpose remained lifelong marriage. Jesus had the right to reaffirm that part of God's purpose in spite of the authority of Moses.

To the question then, 'How are we to describe the Person of Jesus?' the answer, both from the New Testament and the Christian Church, is that He was truly a human being who shared fully in the human condition, and yet the disciples knew that He was God, the eternal 'I AM'.

The other big question that is crucial to any account of Jesus is this:

WHAT DID JESUS DO?

What was His purpose? Of many answers that could be given to that question, two stand out as critical.

☐ *He lived to reveal God to humanity.* There is a story about a little girl who was absorbed in drawing a picture. Her mother asked her what she was drawing. The child replied, 'I'm drawing God.' Her mother smiled and gently pointed out that no one knows what God looks like. The little girl replied impatiently, 'I know that, silly, but they will when I've finished.' It is natural for the child to think of God as a human being on a bigger scale and therefore drawable. She had yet to come to terms with God as 'tremendous mystery' as one theologian put it. And as the French philosopher Blaise Pascal said, 'Define God and He is no longer God.' He meant that God is not akin to observable phenomena which we can investigate, analyse and define.

Yet Pascal believed that God can be known: not by research but by revelation. He was convinced that God has disclosed something of His love and grace through Jesus Christ. The claim of the New Testament is that God has spoken to the world and revealed Himself and His purposes through Jesus Christ. The writer to the Hebrews describes Christ as the Son of God who 'is the radiance of God's glory, the stamp of God's very being' (Hebrews 1:3, REB). It was St Augustine who said that the answer to the mystery of the universe is God, and the answer to the mystery of God is Jesus. Augustine was only echoing what Jesus Himself claimed as His own predestined role as revealer of the Father. In answer to questions put to Him by Thomas and Philip, He said, 'If you knew me you would know my Father too' (John 14:7, REB). Surely the classic example of 'like Father like Son'.

John expresses the same thought at the end of the prologue to the fourth gospel. 'No one has ever seen God; God's only Son, he who is nearest to the Father's heart, has made him known.' (John 1:18, REB.) This is not just high theology. In Jesus' ministry, God's grace is embodied and expressed in many ways. In relieving the embarrassment of a married couple when their wedding celebrations were almost spoiled; in healing the sick and enabling the lame to walk again; in blessing little children; in treating women and men as of equal value; in helping a money-grubber to make a fresh start with different values; in giving His life a ransom for all people; in these and many other ways Jesus made known the heart and mind of God. As John Marsh wrote, 'God remains invisible; the incarnation is not a chance to see God. But He is no longer unknown or unknowable; the mystery of His will and purpose has been made known in the Word who is the Son of God incarnate.' (J. Marsh, *Pelican Commentary on John*, page 112.) In one of the great hymns of the Church, we sing of the Son who reveals the Father:

> *'God hath spoken by Christ Jesus,*
> *Christ, the everlasting Son,*
> *Brightness of the Father's glory,*
> *With the Father ever one;*
> *Spoken by the Word Incarnate,*
> *God of God ere time began,*
> *Light of light, to earth descending*
> *Man, revealing God to man.'*

To the question then, 'What does Jesus do? What is His significance? the first answer is that the New Testament presents Him as a mirror on God the Father: He reveals God. The second major answer to that same question is this:

□ *He died to reconcile humanity to God.* The artist Holman Hunt painted a picture which shows the young Jesus coming to the door of the carpenter's shop in Nazareth and stretching out His arms to ease away the fatigue of a long day at the bench. As the rays of the westering sun fall across His outflung arms they cast a shadow of a cross on the wall behind. By this picture, the artist was saying that Jesus was destined to die. This reflects what is consistently taught in the New Testament. Jesus Himself said that He came into the world to give His life a ransom for many. This accords with the insight given to John the Baptist who declared Jesus to be the Lamb of God who would take away the sin of the world. On the day of Pentecost, Peter told the crowds that the death of Jesus was part of God's plan from the beginning. When the apostle Paul wrote to the Romans, he described the death of Jesus as the proof that God loves us.

Yet some people find the death of Jesus as an atonement a puzzling doctrine. Why, they ask, does God need the death of His Son as a propitiation in order to forgive sins? When human beings forgive one another we do not demand a penance or exact some punishment. Forgiveness is a gracious gift. Why, then, does God not simply forgive on the basis of His grace? Are we greater than God in this respect?

The answer to this thoughtful question lies in the fact that God is the ultimate authority and power in the universe. God is the custodian responsible for upholding standards of right; He is the guarantor that goodness will ultimately prevail; He is the guardian of righteousness. To pardon sin by simply setting aside the moral law would be to undermine that law. Someone might ask at that point: 'Well, if God is God, what prevents Him setting aside the moral law if He should choose to do so? After all, God is surely above the law.' But it is mistaken to think of the moral law as something that can be abstracted from God in that way. We should rather think of the moral law as an expression of God's nature. And if that is the case then God cannot deny Himself by putting the moral law into abeyance. 'If God does not justly punish sin He would be unjust to Himself,' said Anselm of the eleventh century. By the cross of Christ, God can pardon without condoning sin. 'The cross' writes John Stott, 'demonstrates with equal vividness both God's justice in judging sin and His mercy in justifying the sinner. For now, as a result of the pro-pitiatory death of His Son, God can be "just and the justifier" of those who believe in him.' James Denney put it this way: 'God is love, say some, and therefore He dispenses with propitiation. God is love, say the apostles, for He provides the propitiation.'

Another difficulty some feel about the death of Jesus is that it happened so long ago. Can we still think of it as relevant to us? Perhaps that question is best answered with another question. Could anyone claim not to need the forgiveness of God? The evidence in the world around us and the evidence from within us does not suggest that humanity has outgrown the need for forgiveness. In any case, we may be closer to the cross than we realize. We might not have been present at the hill of Calvary, but we were probably well represented there! Recall the kinds of human faults that directly or indirectly caused the sufferings of Christ: there was the disloyalty of Peter, the greed of Judas, the self-preserving pragmatism of Pilate, the manipulative man-oeuvring of Caiaphas, the envy of the Pharisees, the fickleness and sadism of the crowd, the greedy opportunism of the soldiers casting lots for Jesus' garments. These sins, by and large, were fairly ordinary. The people who crucified Jesus were not monsters of evil but a representative cross-section of our humanity. Dr William Sangster said that, 'Christ not only died for my sins, he died by them.' And when the song asks, 'Were you there when they crucified my Lord?' the honest answer is, 'Yes, I was!' And the long passage of time since that event has not severed our link with the cross or our need of it.

The story of Jesus, however, does not end with the darkness of Calvary; it climaxes with the radiant light of Easter morning. The Resurrection on the third day means that Jesus is our ever-living contemporary and we speak of Him always in the present tense; it confirms that Jesus is indeed the Christ, Son of the living God, and that His death was both a revealing of God's love and an atonement for sin. The cross makes us safe, the resurrection makes us sure.

We must end this brief study as we began by admitting that to try to write about Jesus Christ is to realize that our best efforts are inadequate to describe Him. We readily acknowledge with Isaac Watts that the most eloquent portrayals of Him by men or angels,

> *'All are too mean to speak His worth,*
> *Too mean to set my Saviour forth.'*

MARY

A uniquely-favoured person

LUKE 1:28-33

The mother of Jesus Christ, Mary of Nazareth, is undoubtedly the best-known woman in the history of the human race. More has been spoken and written about her than of any other woman. Unfortunately she has also been the subject of much controversial debate among Christians. Those in the Catholic tradition venerate Mary as both a mediator with God on their behalf and their spiritual mother. In the Protestant tradition, Mary is honoured, but only as an ordinary woman chosen by God for the unique honour of being the mother of the Saviour of the world. In this study, we will keep close to the picture of Mary presented in the New Testament.

CHOSEN AND FAVOURED

That Mary was a virtuous and honourable young woman is a widely accepted and fully justified assumption. To begin with, she was a virgin. Admittedly, virginity was prized and guarded jealously in the society to which Mary belonged in a way that would be derided in our society today. Nevertheless, she had kept her virginity, even though she was betrothed to Joseph. Another indication of her piety is the song she composed and recited. We know it as the Magnificat, and in it she reflects deeply on the character of God and His gracious care for the downtrodden and exploited. As further confirmation of her spirituality we note how the angel Gabriel acknowledged that the Lord was with Mary (Luke 1:28). These observations about Mary construct for us a picture of a devout young woman who was considered to be a proper person to be the mother of the Messiah.

And yet the New Testament does not tell us that Mary was given this tremendous honour because she was *worthy* of it. She was chosen and favoured, and it was all a matter of the

19

grace of God. It was the *favour* of God and not the *merit* of Mary that accounts for God's sovereign choice of the young woman from Nazareth. God's favour reflects His goodness not ours. To be His elect is an occasion not for pride but for humility.

Here in the first pages of the New Testament, a principle is established and a pattern laid down: God calls people by His grace to do His will. When the angel says that Mary is 'favoured', he uses a word (Greek: *charitoō*) which means 'to make someone an object of favour'. As Mary did not *qualify* for the honour accorded her, she was made an 'object of favour'. This favour of God is echoed in the affirmation of Elizabeth to Mary, '"God's blessing is on you above all women."' (Luke 1:42, REB.)

Mary was not chosen, therefore, because she was deserving of the honour nor was she chosen so that she might become an illustrious celebrity. She was chosen to serve God's purpose by bearing the Saviour of the world. In this respect Mary's choice is analogous to God's election of the people of Israel who were not elected as the people of God to enjoy a favoured status but, as their finer prophets understood, to be a light to the Gentiles.

God chooses people because He has a purpose for their lives. The apostle Peter makes the same point when he tells his readers that God has called them to be a 'chosen people, a royal priesthood, a holy nation, a people belonging to God', but then he goes on to tell them why God has called them, 'that you may declare the praises of him who called you'. In other words, they were called for their own sakes but just as much for the benefit of others who were to hear their message.

SUBMISSIVE TO HER GOD-ORDAINED DESTINY

Mary herself clearly understood that she was the recipient of God's favour. She responds with humility, '"I am the Lord's servant. . . . May it be to me as you have said."'

(Luke 1:38.) Mary declares herself to be the 'servant' of the Lord. The word used here may be translated 'servant-girl', but the more common use of the Greek word (*doule*) would give the translation 'slave-girl'. It is a strong word indicating Mary's willingness to make her body available to bear a child as the angel had directed. This obedience of Mary's is remarkable for at least four reasons:

□ *It was willing obedience.* It is clear from the way Mary responds to the angel that she knows herself that her consent is required to what is planned for her in the sovereign will of God. We sense at this point that Luke is making it quite clear that Mary's consent is essential. Presumably she could have refused, and would not have been coerced. These words of Mary, therefore, are critical, ' . . . May it be to me as you have said.' It was willing obedience.

Mary's experience exemplifies a paradox or antinomy that runs through the New Testament. An antinomy is defined as the 'contradiction between propositions that seem equally necessary and reasonable; a paradox'. The great paradox implied in God's dealings with people is that He wills and chooses in His sovereignty, yet men and women must freely co-operate. God wills that all people should be saved, but before that can become a reality in a person's life there must be the human response of repentance and faith as the condition for receiving the gift of eternal life. In the same way God may call a person to fulfil a certain role or task, but it is still essential for that person to respond to the call and become available for that role or task.

□ *It was costly obedience.* Mary must have known that consenting to the will of God would place her in an invidious position. How could she explain her pregnancy to Joseph? The future bristled with problems. Bishop Ryle, commenting on this obedience of Mary said, ' . . . it brought with it, no doubt, at a distant period great honour; but it brought with it for the present no small danger to Mary's reputation, and no small trial to Mary's faith'.

Obedience to God's will can be costly. Jesus warned His disciples that in the world they would be persecuted if they followed His way. Discipleship meant taking up a cross daily. And yet, not doing the will of God also has its problems. J. R. Millar wrote, 'It is a great deal easier to do that which God gives us to do, no matter how hard it is, than to face the responsibilities of not doing it.'

□ *It was unconditional obedience.* We cannot say that it was unquestioning obedience since Mary did raise a very sensible question. '"How will this be, since I am a virgin?"' (Luke 1:34.) That was a perfectly reasonable line of questioning. How, indeed, could a virgin bear a child? We note that she was not rebuffed for putting these questions. She was respected and her questions answered. God does not want an unthinking compliance with His will as a robot mechanically carries out the commands of its controller. God looks for the informed obedience of a partner. Of course, the Christian may not always understand the ways of God, but as far as is possible should offer to God a knowledgeable and enlightened obedience.

Given the 'explanation' by the angel, Mary puts no obstacles in the way and accepts her divinely-ordained destiny unconditionally. Our duty is to obey God's directives, not to direct His counsels.

□ *It was instant obedience.* Mary did not ask for a period of time to consider, to think things over. Nor did she ask for an opportunity to consult with Joseph or her family before giving her response. Other people might have attempted to dissuade her from an affirmative reply. Without stalling or temporizing, Mary submitted to God's will. Hers was an obedience promptly given. We may contrast this with the prayer of Augustine before he became a Christian. 'God give me chastity and continency, but not yet.' Delayed obedience is, at least for the time being, disobedience.

AS A MOTHER

There are two things that may be said of Mary as a mother. From the evidence of the New Testament we can safely say that,

☐ *Mary was a good mother.* For thirty years of His life, Jesus was close to His mother. If, as is plausibly conjectured, Joseph had died in Jesus' early teens and Jesus assumed some responsibility for the family, and if the carpenter shop and workshop adjoined their home in Nazareth, then Jesus would inevitably have been close to Mary for much of His earthly life. Luke tells us that Jesus developed as a child and grew 'in wisdom and stature and in favour with God'. His precocious and intelligent questioning of the doctors of the law in the Temple when He was only 12 years old, however much we allow for His own motivation in personal study, must surely reflect the influence of parents and particularly of Mary, for she would be especially conscious of His unique birth and high destiny. Mary must have encouraged the spirituality of the growing boy.

That encouragement may be deduced from two clues. It is almost certain that the family attended the synagogue every Sabbath. This became an established custom of Jesus' life. Luke records that Jesus went to the synagogue in Nazareth 'as he regularly did' (Luke 4:16, REB). This was a habit inculcated in Him from boyhood. The other clue suggesting that Mary encouraged Jesus spiritually is that they took Jesus to Jerusalem for the Feast when He was 12 years old. Devout Jews made the effort to get to Jerusalem for at least one of the three major Feasts. Joseph and Mary went every year for the Passover Festival. As a boy of 12, Jesus attended with his parents in preparation for the following year and His coming of age at 13 (*bar mitzvah*).

As a mother, Mary would not have been able to give Jesus wealth. The family in Nazareth was not rich. How do we know this? Their visit to the Temple when Jesus was presented as a baby gives it away. As part of the post-natal ritual purifying of the mother, a sacrifice was offered. A lamb and a pigeon (or dove) was prescribed, but if the family had limited means a second pigeon might be offered instead of the lamb. This was the option chosen by Mary and Joseph, the option open to the poor. And if, as is believed, Joseph died when Jesus was still young then this would also have had consequences for the income of the family. This is not to suggest they were destitute. In terms of the basic necessities of life they might have been well provided for, but they would not have enjoyed the advantages of wealth.

Mary's gifts to Jesus, however, were more important than wealth. Having given Him the gift of life itself, she went on to give Him the love of a devoted mother, the example of a godly life, the gift of simplicity in lifestyle and a proper sense of values. She encouraged Him to grow in every way — intellectually, physically and spiritually — as we have learned from Luke.

Mary speaks by example to all parents. There are greater gifts than money and material things. The primary gift is love: a poor child who is loved is rich in soul; a wealth-surrounded child who is not loved is poor! Another great gift to pass on to our children is that of a Christian example. Children may ignore advice, but it is harder for them to close their eyes to example. If they see that being a Christian makes their parents into better people, they are more inclined to embrace the faith for themselves. By living according to spiritual values a parent inculcates those same values in the mind of the child.

The other comment that may be made about Mary as a mother is this:

☐ *Mary was not an infallible mother.* Mary was an exemplary mother but she made her mistakes just as other parents do! For example, we read with some surprise that Jesus was lost for three days. After visiting Jerusalem, Mary and Joseph travelled for a whole day on the homeward journey without either of them checking whether their 12-year-old son was in the company. It is possible that Mary thought that Jesus was with

Joseph, and Joseph might have though that He was with Mary. It seems that within the caravan column the women customarily travelled together and so also the men. Younger children usually travelled with their mothers, but older boys might be with mother or father. This may have given rise to the problem, but it does not absolve the parents from blame. During the day's journey they would travel about twenty miles, a long way if they were travelling on foot or on a donkey. Surely they would have ensured that they had all their belongings, but especially their children!

As soon as they discovered that Jesus was not with them, they returned to Jerusalem and eventually found Him in the Temple talking to the doctors of the law. It is Mary who speaks and reprimands Jesus, placing the blame firmly on Him! Obviously, they had learned to expect responsible behaviour from Him. Does the fact that it is Mary and not Joseph who speaks to Jesus mean that Mary felt more responsible? The term she uses to address Him may be significant. She calls Jesus 'child' (Greek: *teknon*) which could be rendered 'my child'. This word *teknon* literally means 'that which is begotten', and its use in this context emphasizes that Mary had borne Jesus and may well be an oblique reference to the virgin birth.

Mary was a good mother as we have seen, but this story shows that she was not infallible. Now to say this is not to demean Mary; in fact most parents will find a stronger affinity with her because she was fallible, since most parents know themselves to be less than perfect. The best of parents make mistakes and looking back over their time as parents, think they could have done better. Mary left Jesus behind not by intent but because she was probably preoccupied. That is a very common problem. How many parents feel that they should have given more time to their children and less to the preoccupations of life?

In Mary's case, however, having slipped up, she did everything to put it right. They searched until they found Him.

Moreover, although she thought Jesus had not treated them as He ought to have done, it made no difference to her commitment to Him as His mother. Greatly relieved, they took Him back to Nazareth and Mary 'treasured up all these things in her heart'. She reflected on what had happened. She learned from the experience. A failure remains a total failure only if we do not learn from it.

AS A DISCIPLE

At some point Mary must have made the transition to being a disciple of Jesus as well as being His mother. We see Mary as disciple in three settings:

□ *At a wedding.* The story is well known. The wine runs out and Mary tells Jesus about the embarrassing situation that has arisen, obviously hoping that He will do something about it. But Jesus adopts an attitude which clearly demonstrates that He is following His Heavenly Father's agenda. He calls Mary 'woman', which is not as rude in Aramaic (used here) as it sounds in English but it does suggest, nevertheless, that His relationship to Mary at this point is that of the Rabbi and disciple. He says to her, '"Why do you involve me?"' (John 2:4.) He adopts an attitude which clearly demonstrates that He has His own agenda.

Mary is a disciple and recognizes the authority of Jesus. She tells the servants at the wedding to '"do whatever he tells you"'. Evidently she is learning to trust and obey Jesus and is encouraging others to obey Him. She believes that whatever the nature of the problem Jesus will be able to help resolve it. She is thinking and functioning as a disciple.

□ *At the cross.* We have seen that Mary became a disciple but she never ceased to be a mother with a mother's love. Nowhere is this more poignantly true than at the crucifixion. Mary was there, close enough so that Jesus could see and know that she was still with Him. Who can plumb the depths of Mary's grief as she watched her son die so cruelly and ignominiously? At Golgotha, Simeon's prophecy about Mary was fulfilled, ' "And a sword will pierce your own soul too." ' (Luke 2:35b.)

Yet even in this scene, what Jesus says to Mary is a strange mixture of a son talking to His mother and the Master talking to His disciple. By addressing Mary as 'woman', Jesus speaks as the Master. But by commending her to John He shows a deep filial concern for her as His mother. There is no justification for the view that because Jesus told Mary to regard John as her son Mary was thus set apart as a kind of universal mother to all Christians. It does mean, however, that Jesus was ensuring that Mary would be part of another disciple's household. At this stage, as far as we can tell, Jesus' half brothers were not disciples; so, by appointing John to serve as an 'adopted' son, Jesus knew that His mother would be encouraged and supported after His death in a way that her other sons would not be capable of at that juncture.

□ *At a prayer meeting.* The last time we see Mary in the New Testament she is with the disciples in the upper room (Acts 1:14), prior to the day of Pentecost. By now the brothers of Jesus are with her and they are part of the Christian community. Herbert Lockyer suggested that Mary herself might have influenced her family to abandon their misgivings about Jesus and 'led them into a full-orbed faith'. If this conjecture is correct, then Mary emerges as a role-model for Christian parents in the way she encouraged her sons to believe in and follow Jesus, and to join in the meeting of the disciples. This last glimpse of Mary in the New Testament shows her as a member of the Christian group, closely associated with the apostles, joining in prayer and encouraging her family.

In this study we have kept close to what the New Testament has said about Mary and avoided comment on the Mary of post-biblical Church dogma. From this exclusively New Testament vantage point we have seen that Mary was uniquely favoured, an exemplary if fallible mother, a loyal disciple, and a member of the embryonic Church. These are, therefore, good reasons for all Christians to honour Mary, both as the mother of Jesus and for the example of faith, love and obedience she has set before us.

PETER

The man with a new name to live up to
JOHN 1:42

When we think of the twelve apostles of Christ, the first name that comes to mind will probably be that of Simon Peter. His ebullient nature and impetuosity made it inevitable that he would be visible in many of the incidents recorded in the New Testament. This high profile is reflected in the fact that his name always appears first in the lists of the disciples.

WHAT'S IN A NAME?

It is not surprising if the names by which Peter is known cause some confusion. For one thing, we are dealing with four languages: Hebrew (Simeon), Aramaic (Cephas), Greek (Petros), and English (Peter). The name given to him by his parents was Simeon, but this had been shortened to Simon 'as a Greek name of similar sound'. The Hebrew purist might still call him Simeon — as, indeed, the apostles did later in Jerusalem (Acts 15:14).

When Andrew brought Simon, his brother, to Jesus, Jesus said, '"You are Simon son of John. You will be called Cephas" (which, when translated, is Peter).' (John 1:42.) Jesus renamed Simon and called him Cephas. Now Cephas is Aramaic for 'rock'. But why, in that case, was he not known as Cephas? The reason for that goes back to Alexander the Great who, in his many conquests, spread the Greek language extensively over the known world. Greek was the *lingua franca* and so it was that Peter was called by the Greek word for rock, Petros. In English, Petros becomes Peter.

In calling Simon a 'rock' Jesus was saying something like this: 'Follow Me, Simon, and you will become rocklike in your character: stable, strong and dependable.' Jesus was placing before him an image of the kind of person he was intended and destined to become by the grace of God. The name, rock, did not reflect the character of Simon as he then was: it was much more a projection of what he was to become; it was not descriptive but predictive. It was as if Jesus could see two Simons: a present and a future version. The present Simon possessed a rather volatile temperament; he was a man with leadership potential but unpredictable and impulsive. The future Simon would be a strong and stable person, a true *Petros*.

As time passed, there were occasions when an impetuous outburst or an inappropriate response to something Jesus said made the name 'rock' seem a misnomer. He could be so unrocklike! He made and broke a promise with the same vigour. He promised Jesus, 'Though all men fail you, yet I will not fail you.' Within a short time of making that bold profession of superior loyalty, he denied ever knowing Jesus — and even treacherous Judas never denied being a disciple. Yet, in spite of failures, the name Peter stayed with him. Every time someone addressed him by name the word 'rock' would remind him of the kind of person he was intended to be.

Peter, then, was challenged by his new name; it was a name to live up to. Every Christian is in the same position, with a name to live up to. To call oneself a 'Christian' is to say 'I belong to Christ'. The name Christian might be literally rendered 'Christ's one'. There may be times in our lives when the name Christian seems a distinctly optimistic description; times when by our behaviour we may feel that we have forfeited all right to the name. Nevertheless, in the grace of God we keep the name, for it is by grace 'we are saved', and in His great patience God does not cast us aside. As Jesus persevered with Peter, so God bears with us: forgiving, restoring, guiding, admonishing and inspiring all who keep following — as Peter kept following in spite of his failures.

VIVID CONTRASTS

H. G. Wells said of one of his characters, Mr Polly, 'He was not so much a human being as a civil war.' It may be overstating the case to say that Peter was a civil war, but he certainly was capable of acting as though he had several different selves. The words that came from Peter's mouth on various occasions seemed not to come from the same source. In a searching passage in his epistle, James wrote about the power of the tongue as a power for good and a power for mischief. He wrote, 'Out of the same mouth come praise and curses.' (James 3:10.) Peter would have agreed with James, no doubt ruefully admitting that he was guilty of doing what James warns his readers against: his mouth had uttered praises and curses.

We can recall the time when Peter spoke great words of wisdom and praise. When large numbers of people deserted Jesus He turned to His disciples and asked, 'Will you also go away?' It was Peter who saw how foolish and shortsighted it would be to leave Christ. 'Lord,' he responded, 'to whom shall we go? You have the words of eternal life.' Peter was saying that those who renounced Jesus were not only being disloyal; they were also acting against their own best interests. Peter was here both acknowledging the authority of Jesus and encouraging the other disciples. Peter's mouth could, indeed, speak forth praise.

Or take another example of the good that came out of Peter's mouth. One day Jesus asked the disciples, '"Who do you say that I am?"' (Matt. 16:15.) It was Peter who gave an answer. 'You are the Christ, the Son of the living God.' Jesus said that this reply of Peter's was inspired by God. Peter was the first to discover that Jesus was the Messiah of Hebrew prophecy. Yes, there were times when Peter could speak with the tongue of an angel.

Yet the same voice that confessed Jesus to be the Messiah also denied and disowned the Lord. To make the denial more convincing he 'swore' that he did not know Jesus. This we may take to mean that Peter reinforced his treacherous disavowal with a sworn oath. He also called down curses on himself if he was not telling the truth. Peter did not do anything by half!

It is difficult to believe that we are dealing with the same person; the one who, at Caesarea Philippi, confessed the Messianic status of Jesus, and the one who, in the courtyard of Caiaphas, denied he ever knew Jesus. Yet, if we are honest, most of us would be willing to agree that we are not as constant or as consistent as we should like to think we are. It may be that Peter is such a popular disciple because people can identify with him. There was nothing unique about Peter. Most of us would admit that there is too much of Peter's inconsistency in our commitment and devotion to allow us to point an accusing finger at him. Robert Browning expressed these contradictions in the self, thus:

> 'Sadly mixed natures: self-indulgent, yet
> self-sacrificing too: now the love
> Soars, now the craft, avarice, vanity and spite —
> and we sink again.'

Yet no one should despair of these contradictions, at least, not if the example of Peter is anything to go by.

ON TO MATURITY

As we follow Peter's progress in the New Testament, we can trace how he became stable in character. His example shows clearly that whereas a decision to follow Christ may be taken quickly, growing in stature as a Christian, becoming more Christlike, producing the 'fruit of the Spirit' (Gal. 5:22, 23), and generally becoming more 'rocklike' and dependable, will take longer.

☐ *Factors in Peter's growth.* How are we to account for the growth in Peter?

First there was the patient forgiveness of Jesus. After Peter's denial, he did not meet with Jesus again until after the resurrection. His sense of desolation at the death of his Master must have been exacerbated by a deep feeling of self-recrimination, perhaps self-loathing. How could he ever face

Jesus again? Was a reconciliation possible after that disgraceful display of disloyalty in the courtyard? Would Jesus forgive him and give him another chance?

The response from Jesus was expressed in two ways. *He wanted to talk to Peter.* Mark tells us that 'the young man', generally taken to be an angel, who spoke to the women at the tomb, gave them a message for the apostles, and Peter was mentioned specifically. '"But go, tell his disciples and Peter, 'He is going ahead of you into Galilee. There you will see him, as he told you.'"' (Mark 16:7.) ' . . . *and Peter.*' They were to make sure that Peter got the message that Jesus wanted him to be there! True forgiveness means a restoration of a relationship and not simply the cancelling of the wrong. Here is a model for our forgiving one another. It will never be enough to say, 'I will forgive the person who has wronged me but the relationship between us can never be the same again.' That is not the way Jesus treated Peter. He particularly wanted to see Peter so that the relationship could be perfectly restored.

Jesus' response to Peter's failure was expressed in a second way. *He was willing to trust Peter.* Jesus did not take the attitude that having failed under pressure Peter could not be trusted again. In that well-known interview on the shores of Galilee recorded in the fourth gospel (John 21:15-19), Jesus invited Peter to reaffirm his love by becoming a shepherd to the flock of God. This meant that Peter, in spite of his denials, was still an apostle, was still in the service of the King. He had expressed a real repentance moments after he denied Jesus (Matt. 26:75) and now he was being reinstated to the work for which he had been called. This confidence which Jesus showed in Peter would restore his sense of self-worth and give him the courage to go forward.

But there was also need for Peter to be willing to learn from failure, and this learning from failure would be another factor in his growth to maturity. Experience is a great teacher, and if we are good students in the school of life we shall learn from our mistakes. Dr Samuel Smiles observed, 'We learn wisdom much more from failure than from success. We often discover what *will* do by finding out what *will not* do; and probably he who never made a mistake never made a discovery.' Failure is never a pleasant experience, but it need not be totally negative if we learn valuable lessons from it.

Secondly, there were two other factors which had a decisive effect on Peter's life as he moved on to maturity. The resurrection of Christ resolved for him, as it did for the other disciples, those somewhat enigmatic sayings of Jesus about His own future, and gave Peter a new dimension of confidence in God and in God's power. He would now believe that God's purpose could not be frustrated. This would have a tremendously stabilizing effect on Peter. The other event that had a great impact upon Peter was the coming of the Holy Spirit at Pentecost. In the New Testament, the Holy Spirit is described as the Enabler, the Enlightener, the Guide into all truth, the Sanctifier, to name but a few of the ways the Spirit is said to influence the believer. As we follow Peter's life, there is good reason to believe that he grew strong as he was guided and empowered by the Holy Spirit.

☐ *Evidence of Peter's growth.* What evidence is there to confirm that peter *did* grow in Christian character? Did he become the *petros* Jesus predicted when He gave him the name? His leadership during the early days of the Church provides a strong indication of such development in Peter. The Acts of the Apostles gives us two incontrovertible pieces of evidence, illustrating how different Peter became as he grew 'in grace and the knowledge' of Christ.

First Peter moved from fear-driven denial to courageous witness. The courage Peter had displayed in the garden when he cut off the ear of the servant of the High Priest deserted him when he was alone in the courtyard of Caiaphas. The craven fear he felt as he warmed himself by the fire drove him to disown Jesus, and probably left him feeling that he was the world's biggest coward.

Some time later, Peter was himself arrested and spent a

night in gaol. The next morning he was brought before the Sanhedrin (Acts 4) and asked for an explanation of the miracle that had been performed at the Gate Beautiful. In response Peter spoke with great boldness, quite unashamed now to identify himself with Jesus to whose powerful Name he attributed the miracle. And when he was told to stop talking about Jesus Christ, Peter refused to be intimidated and said that he intended obeying God and not men. We can discern in Peter a growing strength in his character.

Secondly, another aspect of Peter's character that needed to be sorted out was his impetuosity. As we meet him in the Gospels, there is a certain volatility about his nature, a certain lack of self-restraint, a tendency to speak and then think. Before he could become a 'rock' he would need to cultivate self-restraint; before he could lead others he would need to control himself. Is there any evidence that Peter did become, by the grace of God, more temperate? The great Council of Jerusalem recorded in Acts chapter fifteen gives us a glimpse of a more self-controlled Peter. We read with some surprise that Peter is one of the last to speak, or at least he has given everyone else an opportunity to speak. Luke reports, 'After much discussion, Peter got up and addressed them . . . .' (Acts 15:7.) There was a time when Peter would have been on his feet before anyone else, pontificating, dogmatizing and generally dominating the proceedings. Now he waits, listens to others, and only then does he make a strong plea against imposing circumcision on Gentiles. His intervention was critical and virtually settled the matter. Peter is still a strong character but it is now harnessed strength. As we mark his conduct in the Council of Jerusalem, the old impetuosity is under control, and by now we are able to say of him, 'Rock by name and rock by nature.'

As we think of Peter in relation to this name *rock*, a final question arises: Was he the rock on which the Church was to be built? What did Jesus mean when He said to Peter, '"You are Peter, and on this rock I will build by church"'? (Matt. 16:18.) William Barclay called this passage 'one of the storm-centres of New Testament interpretation'. It is a passage which sharply divides Roman Catholic and Protestant exegetes. So far as Catholics are concerned, Peter was assigned unique and singular powers by this statement of Jesus, powers that would pass down from Pope to Pope as successors of Peter.

The difficulty with this interpretation is that the New Testament from the Acts of the Apostles onwards does not itself accord any unique authority to the apostle Peter. Certainly, he was one of the prominent leaders and would be greatly respected because of his nearness to Jesus. Among other apostles, however, he was simply one of the leaders. Even those who did regard him as the most prominent of the apostles would probably think of him as *primus inter pares*. At the Council of Jerusalem, although Peter's contribution, as we have noted, was crucial to the outcome of the debate, it was James who appears to have presided on that occasion and it was James who proposed the formula which was adopted. The letter embodying the findings of the Council was sent, not under the imprimatur of an authoritative Peter, but 'from the apostles and elders . . . '.

We may further note that when Peter stopped taking meals with Gentile Christians at Antioch (Gal. 2:11, 12), Paul 'opposed him to his face, because he was in the wrong'. If there had been a general understanding that Peter was uniquely invested with the government of the Church, would Paul have spoken to him in the way he did?

The letter to the Ephesians seems to rule out the theory that the Church was to be built on Peter: 'You are . . . built on the foundation of the apostles and prophets, with Christ Jesus himself as the chief corner-stone.' (Eph. 2:20.) And what is particularly interesting is that Peter himself, using a Messianic passage from Isaiah (28:16), describes Christ as '"'. . . a corner-stone of great worth.'"' (1 Peter 2:6, NEB.) In the first

Corinthian letter, Paul inveighed against the Corinthians for their faction-creating practice of championing one apostle above the others (1 Cor. 1:12).

If, then, we cannot take the statement of Jesus to mean that Peter was to be the foundation of the Church, how are we to read it? Three explanations are possible. (1) It is Peter's affirmation that Jesus is the Messiah and the Son of God, the God-given revelation, upon which the Church will be built. (2) The second explanation does admit that Jesus had Peter in mind, but not as the rock on which the Church was to be founded but as the initial stone. Everyone who makes 'the same discovery as Peter', wrote William Barclay, 'is another stone into the edifice of the Church of Christ'. In other words we do not think of Peter in terms of primacy, but as the first disciple fully to confess Jesus as the Messiah and the Son of God. (3) The third explanation is that Jesus was gesturing towards Peter when He said, 'Thou art Peter', but towards Himself when He said, 'but upon this Rock will I build by Church' (a play on words).

What we read of Peter on the Gospel page reveals the immense patience of Jesus in persevering with a person who blew hot and cold; a follower so bold in his protestations of loyalty yet who was so vulnerable under pressure. The patience of Jesus was rewarded. Peter learned from his mistakes, received forgiveness, forgave himself, grew progressively more steady in his own character, and developed a sensitive deference to others. Peter lived up to his name: Simeon became a rock.

MATTHEW
The unlikely apostle
MATTHEW 9:9-13; LUKE 5:27-32

Matthew enjoys the unique privilege of having his name at the top of the first page of the New Testament, and he has attained this honour in spite of the fact that when Jesus called him he was anything but an ideal candidate for the apostolate. It is no exaggeration to say that anyone other than Jesus would have looked elsewhere than among the ranks of the tax collectors for a potential apostle.

Matthew was a tax collector, and the fact that he worked in a booth on the highway suggests that he was a kind of customs officer in the district of Galilee. His task would be to collect taxes on all kinds of goods. Howard Marshall describes Matthew as a 'subordinate official engaged in the actual collection of the tolls for a tax farmer'.

Tax collectors were universally disliked and despised. The only friend Matthew would have would be another tax collector. According to William Barclay 'of all the nations the Jews were the most vigorous haters of tax collectors'. The Pharisees had no compunction in characterizing the tax collector as a 'sinner'. Why did they have such a bad reputation? The system itself was wide open to abuse by those who operated it. Each region had a Tax Contractor. He was usually a Roman who, by offering the highest bid to Rome, secured the right to gather the taxes of a particular area. In practice, it turned out to be private enterprise of the most exploitative kind. The Contractor would appoint men to do the actual collecting and the tax levels were set at a rate that would ensure a big profit. The fact that tax collectors were generally very rich confirmed the widespread opinion that the tax collectors were abusing the system. Jews who helped to operate this corrupt 'civil service' were considered to be the lowest of the low. Matthew was such a man and to most of his fellow Jews he was *persona non grata*, a man who had sold his birthright and betrayed his people for material gain.

At this point a question arises. If Matthew was the typically hardened materialist these taxmen were reputed to be, why did he respond so readily to someone like Jesus? It seems incredible that Matthew should leave all and follow a man who was well known for his 'bias to the poor'. We are left to conjecture. It may be that the magnetic personality of Jesus was sufficient to draw him. It is more likely that an inner ferment caused by discontentment and disillusionment with his way of life had partly prepared Matthew for the call from Jesus. For all its obvious uses, had money failed to bring the happiness and fulfilment Matthew craved? Was he haunted by a sense of guilt because of the immoral means by which he had grown rich? Did he wistfully yearn, in more thoughtful moments, for a new way of life? If so, the call of Jesus opened a door for Matthew into a new life and he took the opportunity.

It may be that Matthew's example is an encouragement to Christians who are seeking to win others for Christ. Many people like Matthew seem impervious to the Gospel and appear to be totally preoccupied with materialistic pursuits with no interest in the things of God. That is how many people would have felt about Matthew; he was not the 'type' to be interested in faith and spiritual matters. But that would have been a mistaken judgement based only on outward image; in his heart he was probably ripe for the call from Christ.

So far as the call of Jesus to Matthew is concerned we may note:

HE RESPONDED WITHOUT HESITATION

According to Luke's version of the story Matthew promptly 'left all, rose up and followed Jesus'. Was Matthew reacting impulsively? There is always the danger that anything done on the spur of the moment and without proper forethought will simply prove to have been a flash in the pan. A decision taken easily might be changed just as easily! But there was nothing shallow or short-lived about Matthew's commitment. In the years that followed, there was no wavering or turning back. He was aware that when Jesus came his way it was a moment of destiny for him. We remember the words of Shakespeare:

> 'There is a tide in the affairs of men,
> Which, taken at the flood, leads on to fortune.'

The Bard is saying that there is a moment of opportunity that must not be missed. And for Matthew something more than Shakespeare's fortune was at stake. He needed peace with God, peace with his own conscience, peace with others and a more worthy purpose to live for. When the call came from Jesus, Matthew sensed that the door of opportunity was opened before him; he strode through it gladly and never looked back.

Matthew reminds us of the urgency of a prompt response when Christ calls us to discipleship. There is almost a paradox in the call of Christ. He asks for a thoughtful response with a full awareness of what is involved in being a disciple (Luke 9:57, 58). Yet He calls men and women to follow without delay. The two men in the gospel who wanted to postpone their commitment to discipleship (Luke 9:59-61) offered different excuses, but neither reason was accepted. Augustine once said, 'It's never too early to begin to follow Christ but at any moment it could be too late.' And it was Augustine who made the same point when he said, 'God has promised forgiveness to your repentance, but He has not promised tomorrow to your procrastination.' The offer of forgiveness and entry into the Kingdom of God is not withdrawn; it is there through all our life on earth. The danger of procrastination is largely on our side. If a person does not respond to the call of Christ in the moment of opportunity, the demands made upon him in his daily life and the tendency for life to get ever more busy may erode the desire and willingness to respond. Matthew sets the right example in his prompt response.

Soon after Matthew had committed himself as a follower of Christ, he threw a big party and invited many guests, including Jesus and His disciples. It might have been a bit reckless on the part of Matthew to spend what resources he had on a feast. He had, after all, abandoned the lucrative tax collecting; he would certainly not get rich as one of the twelve disciples. A more cautious approach might have persuaded him to be more prudent, what with all the financial uncertainty that would now be a part of his life as a disciple, compared with his life as a tax collector. But was this feast an indication of a change in Matthew: the grasping hand is now opened to give? Does he have a changed attitude to money that does not see it as the be-all and end-all of life? Why did Matthew give this 'Dinner Party' as we might call it? There were probably three reasons:

☐ *Matthew wanted to celebrate.* Sharing a meal has long been, and still is, the preferred way to celebrate important events in our lives. Matthew felt that a new way of life was opening up before him and he was excited about it. He was casting off the odious occupation that had made him an outcast; he was embarking upon a new adventure in company with the remarkable Jesus of Nazareth. Matthew wanted to celebrate and express his gratitude and joy by throwing this feast for his friends.

Matthew's feast stands in the gospel as a symbol of joy and gladness found in following Christ; something to celebrate with a party! Many people have the mistaken notion that Christianity is a sombre kind of life, exclusively preoccupied with restrictions and self-denial. Now it is perfectly true that there are what might be termed negative commands in the Judeo-Christian tradition, but these are calculated not to diminish true freedom but to protect and enhance it. The command not to steal is a negative rule, but when it is honoured will have positive consequences for the individual and society.

As Matthew rejoiced in the new life opening before him, his instinct was to celebrate. And it needs to be said that a feast, perhaps more than a fast, is a symbol of Christianity. When Billy Bray, a Cornishman, was converted he said that the whole world looked different: the hedgerows, the cattle in the fields, the whole of nature. And long before Billy Bray, Francis of Assisi said, 'Sadness belongs to the devil and his angels, but we, believing what we believe, and knowing what we know, what can we do, except rejoice?' It may be that Christians need to be reminded of something Ruskin once said, 'We are converted, not to long and gloomy faces, but to round and laughing ones.' Jesus said that He had come so that those who believe in Him 'might have life, and . . . have it more abundantly' (John 10:10, KJV).

A second reason for Matthew's feast was this:

☐ *He wanted to invite Jesus into his home.* We do not know what family Matthew had. We can safely assume he had a wife and probably children. Every Jewish man was expected to marry and produce a family. Matthew clearly wanted to create an opportunity, by way of this dinner party, for his family to meet Jesus. Was Matthew, having dedicated himself to the service of Christ, now consecrating his home also to be a place where Christ would be honoured and obeyed? If so, then he is setting a challenging example to all who follow Christ. Matthew was willing to have Jesus in his home; he was willing for his home to be a place where the things of God were talked about; he was willing for his home to be a place where enquirers would find a welcome.

But, most important of all, Matthew was indicating that he wanted to be a disciple in his own home, and home is not always the easiest place to be a disciple. There used to be a saying in former times, 'No man is a hero to his valet.' Why not? His valet knew him and observed his conduct and behaviour when all the polite façade of social etiquette was laid aside with the dinner suit and 'my lord' was truly himself. How a Christian conducts himself or herself at home is a critical test of the genuineness of his or her Christianity. Matthew takes his discipleship home. He wanted the kingdom of God to come in his home. The following prayer was spotted at the entrance to a house:

> 'O God make the door of this house wide enough to
> receive all who need human love and fellowship, narrow
> enough to shut out all envy, pride and strife. Make
> its threshold smooth enough to be no stumbling block,
> but rugged and strong enough to turn back the tempter's
> power. God make the door of this house the gateway to
> thine eternal kingdom, through Jesus Christ our Lord,
> Amen.'

That prayer was written long after Matthew's time but it expresses what Matthew had in mind: to create a home where Christ was welcome and build a family based on Christian values.

A third reason why Matthew made this feast was this:

☐ *Matthew wanted to introduce other people to Jesus.* The meal Matthew arranged would provide a pleasant and relaxed setting away from the jostling crowds, a setting in which his own family and his tax colleagues could meet Jesus for themselves. However, the sight of all those tax collectors gathered in one place to sit at table in the company of Jesus and His disciples was more than the Pharisees could stomach. They aimed one of their broadsides at the disciples for sitting down with a swarm of swindlers; to them it made Matthew's house look like a veritable thieves' kitchen. So far as the Pharisees were concerned, the tax collectors were hopeless cases; in terms of religion and morality, beyond redemption. But this was not the way Jesus looked upon them. He was 'the one who came, ruined sinners to reclaim'. In fact, these 'sinners' might prove to be more responsive to the call of Christ to 'repent and believe' than some of the Pharisees who self-righteously believed themselves to be spiritually wealthy with 'no need of a physician'. The tax collectors, by contrast, would be well aware of the corruption in their profession so that it might not be too difficult to convince them of the need for forgiveness and a new beginning.

Perhaps Matthew, with his close knowledge of his former colleagues, knew that some of them were disillusioned with their way of life, ill at ease with themselves as Zacchaeus seemed to have been, and were wanting a better and nobler life that would bring them inner peace. Matthew had found that new way in Jesus Christ, and he wanted to share his news with his former friends and maybe see some of them share the peace and sense of purpose he was finding in following Jesus. There can be little doubt that this feast was intended by Matthew to be a witness and if we see it in that light it has much to teach us about witnessing.

We note that as an exercise in witness it was *in deed as well as in word*. Matthew displays his generosity by inviting people to a meal and that meal typifies the need for a practical ministry to other people that will confirm the witness made in words. The hospitality of his home and the generous provision would itself be part of Matthew's witness. The story is told of a young German pastor who accepted a call in the 1930s to a church in a village where few people attended church. He preached and visited with almost no response. Then one day he called to see a women who suffered from ulcerated legs. Her plight was so distressing that the pastor removed the bandages and did what he could to treat the condition. News of the pastor's kindness spread through the village, and the next Sunday more people than usual attended worship and his congregation began to grow. The concern he showed to someone in need touched the hearts of the people, and they became more inclined to listen to his message. When the 'Word was made flesh and dwelt among us' God spoke to the world in word but also in deed, in the incarnate life in Christ.

This feast given by Matthew as an exercise in witness *was Christ-centred*. Its aim was to introduce others to Jesus. Whatever methods are employed in evangelism, the underlying aim is always the same, to enable people to meet the Saviour; the ultimate goal of evangelism has not been attained until that happens. Matthew's method was a meal, but it was to be an opportunity also for people to meet Jesus. This does not mean that Matthew's feast was simply a ruse to get them there, as a carrot entices the donkey to move forward; he meant them to enjoy a meal, but he needed to explain the change of direction his life had taken, and he could think of no better way. When the Church offers aid to the needy it is not done with a view to 'softening' people up for the Gospel; the aid should be given as an act of Christian caring without strings or conditions, but neither is it an alternative or substitute for speaking about Jesus Christ. True witness is in deed and in word, in word and in deed. The Church's mandate which is enshrined in the great commission given by Christ is to preach the Gospel in all the world.

MATTHEW AS WRITER

Let it be admitted that there are a number of scholars who do not accept the Matthean authorship of the first gospel. Yet a reference to the gospel in the early centuries of the Church by Papias (c. 60-130), Bishop of Hierapolis, who was said to have heard John the apostle; and a reference by Irenaeus, Bishop of Lyons in the last quarter of the second century, who had links with the apostolic generation through Polycarp; and a reference in Origen (c. 185-254) all attribute the gospel to the apostle Matthew. The late Dr Donald Guthrie, after a careful analysis of the data and taking full account of the difficulties, could write, ' . . . there is no conclusive reason for rejecting the strong external testimony regarding the authorship of Matthew . . . .' (*New Testament Introduction*, Tyndale, 1965, page 42.) He goes on to suggest that the attention to detail which would be essential for a tax collector's bookkeeping may be reflected in the methodological structure of the gospel. If this is the case, it is an interesting example of a disciple's using an acquired skill in the service of Christ.

Matthew has his own distinct emphases. For example, he accentuates the Messianic role of Jesus in whose life Jewish prophecy is fulfilled. This explains the large number of quotations from the Old Testament, and it illustrates Matthew's concern to demonstrate that Jesus was no maverick, no iconoclast, no schismatic but the One whose coming was foretold by Jewish prophets.

On a personal level, this must have meant that Matthew possessed a vivid sense of being a subject of the King, a subject of great David's greater Son. For Matthew that would mean a true king, not just the modern figurehead version of a king, a constitutional monarch, as the name connotes today, but the divine King, with authority and power over the lives of His subjects. For the Christian, therefore, to call Christ by the name King much more is involved than a vague recognition that at some time in the future He will be manifest in majesty, power, and glory. Wherever Jesus is truly acknowledged as King, the allegiance offered to Him is altogether more personal and spiritual than the loyalty that is offered to an earthly monarch. Only an obedience that is complete, involving heart, mind and will, can be regarded as a worthy service to bring to the King of kings. Josiah Conder expresses the crown rights of Christ in his great hymn:

'The Lord is King! who then shall dare
resist His will, distrust His care,
or murmur at His wise decrees,
or doubt His royal promises.'

We have noted from the limited references to Matthew in the New Testament that when he was called to follow Jesus he allowed nothing to delay an immediate and affirmative response. Matthew was not ashamed or hesitant about committing himself as a disciple. He was prepared radically to revise his sense of values, and in particular his attitude to money. Matthew considered his new-found discipleship something to be joyously celebrated. He was eager to introduce both his family and his former colleagues to Christ. Finally, he has reminded us that Jesus Christ is the Messiah King who requires loyal and wholehearted allegiance from those of us who know that by obedience to His wise leadership we find greatest freedom and fulfilment.

MARY MAGDALENE

A devoted disciple

LUKE 8:1-3

The woman known as Mary Magdalene is a prominent disciple in the New Testament. What appears to us to be her surname — Magdalene — is really a nickname. It means 'of Magdala'. Mary was identified, therefore, by the name of her home town, just as we speak of Helen of Troy, Augustine of Hippo, and so on. Maybe the name Mary was a common one at that time, as it certainly was in the New Testament, and this was a way of distinguishing this particular Mary, the Mary from Magdala.

It is interesting that this long-forgotten town on the shores of Galilee has been immortalized in the nickname of its most famous daughter. As we attempt now to review what may be learned about Mary in the New Testament we shall discover that she was, indeed, a devoted disciple.

SLANDERED BY A MISINTERPRETATION

There has been a strong tradition that Mary was a prostitute before she became a disciple of Jesus, yet there is no biblical justification for this at all. Why then, did the idea arise? What are the reasons for believing that Mary was a harlot?

□ Some commentators have identified Mary with the unnamed woman 'who was a sinner' in Luke 7:37. The only reason for linking Mary with this 'sinner' is that Mary is mentioned first in the passage in the next chapter that immediately follows the story about the sinner. This is a totally arbitrary and unwarranted conclusion. In any case, there are two other women, Joanna and Susanna, who are mentioned with Mary. Why are they not linked with 'the sinner'?

□ The Jewish Ta'mud claims that Magdala had an unsavoury

reputation and its destruction was a judgement on the amount of prostitution that was allowed in the town. Commentators have extrapolated from the town's bad name and surmised that Mary was one of the harlots. Does this not tarnish Mary without sufficient evidence?

☐ Mark and Luke tell us that Jesus cast seven evil spirits from Mary. Some commentators connected the seven demons to the seven deadly sins and argued that Mary must have been a particularly evil person; and so they felt justified in identifying her with the woman who was a sinner. The codifying of seven deadly sins, however, came later in the history of the Church; so the link with the seven evil spirits is anachronistic. I. Howard Marshall makes the point that 'demon possession and sinfulness are to be carefully distinguished'.

Because of this misunderstanding, Mary has often been held up as an example of the power of Christ to save prostitutes. And it may be the case that women rescued from an immoral life have found inspiration from the fact that Mary is so prominent in the New Testament, in spite of her alleged background in prostitution. An order of nuns called the Magdalens was established in the Roman Church by Pope Leo X (sixteenth century). The order was comprised mainly of women who had been rescued from harlotry. Yes, of course, the truth about the love of God for prostitutes should be affirmed, but not by defaming Mary.

This harlot reputation has provided those who staged 'Jesus Christ Superstar' with an opportunity — an opportunity usually avidly grasped — to create a voluptuous Mary in the cast of the musical. She supplies the erotic dimension.

Christian feminists are justified in their contention that this portrayal of Mary, created by men, has helped to perpetuate the myth that women are more prone to sexual weakness and temptation than men. In a reference to Mary Magdalene and the caricature of women by male writing, Elizabeth Moltmann-Wendel says, '*The* figure of biblical womanhood has the past of a sinner.' Deploring this fact she insists that

'Mary Magdalene must again become the woman with her own personal history, rather than being the prototype of the sinful woman'.

LIBERATED FOR A NEW LIFE

Both Mark and Luke tell us that Mary was set free by Jesus from seven demons. The demon-possessed person's general condition would resemble mental affliction; there would be a loss of control over mind and body, leading to a sense of hopelessness and despair. In this condition, suicide would often seem to be the only exit from the relentless torment.

This was Mary's sad plight when she came into contact with Jesus. He exorcised the demons and transformed the situation for Mary, opening for her the door to a new life. To use biblical language, we might say that salvation had come to Mary as Jesus once said it came to Zacchaeus. What did salvation mean in Mary's experience?

☐ *She received the forgiveness of God.* We have seen that there is no evidence to suggest that Mary was a harlot. Nevertheless, it is entirely possible that by her former mode of life she had made herself susceptible to evil powers. She might have experimented with occultic practices, or she might have consorted with people whose baleful influence led her astray. In some way, she might have predisposed herself to possession, and in that case she would need to be forgiven and to make a break with the past. Healing and forgiveness go together in the ministry of Jesus.

Forgiveness may be the most important aspect of wholeness. One of the Greek verbs used for forgiveness was also used of a horse about to set off in a race. It was released to fulfil what it was trained to do. Forgiveness frees people into that potential which God our Creator has placed within us. We are released by forgiveness as Mary was released.

☐ *She regained control over her life.* Her condition previously had been marked by a loss of control. Other examples of demon possession in the New Testament bear this out. Set free by Jesus, Mary would feel that she was a true person again, exhilarated to be in control over her own mind and body. She found that in following Jesus Christ she had been liberated from bondage. That is the paradox of Christian discipleship: living under the Lordship of Christ a person finds true freedom.

There are many kinds of bondage in the world today, and words such as 'addicted', 'dependent', and 'hooked' are in common currency. Yet drugs are not the only bondage. Ovid wrote, 'I see the right and approve of it, I see the wrong and abhor it, but it is the wrong I do.' Jesus Christ sets a person free from the inner constraints of sin.

☐ *She rediscovered the ability to relate to others.* Another feature of her previous condition was that it must have isolated her from people, and maybe even from her own family. The mental instability associated with her condition would have made meaningful relationships difficult. This all changed for Mary, however, when she came under the influence and power of Jesus. The new Mary was able to mix freely with the disciples and become a member of the band of women who acted as a support group to Jesus and the disciples in their travels.

There is a sense in which the changes Jesus Christ effects in the lives of all who follow Him should enable them to be better at making and keeping relationships. In the lives of those who are open to His saving power, He will cast out the spirit of selfishness and the spirit of unforgiveness; He will exorcize old grudges and prejudices and He will introduce those lives to a new concept of love, which is the secret of the most rewarding and lasting relationships.

☐ *She rejoiced in a new purpose.* In one of His parables, Jesus warned that it is not enough to cast the demons out and leave it at that. That would only create a vacuum. There is a well-known saying, 'Nature abhors a vacuum'; every gardener knows that if you do not fill the empty space with plants the weeds will soon take over. This principle is true so far as a faith in God is concerned. G. K. Chesterton once said, 'When men cease to believe in God they don't believe in nothing, they will believe in anything.' Mary avoided the problem of the vacuum by becoming immediately involved as a helper in the work Jesus was doing. She found a new purpose to life.

Mary was not without resources. Dr Herbert Lockyer suggested that she might have been connected at one time with the industry of Magdala. There were 'dye works and primitive textile factories' in the town. Whatever the source of her wealth it appears that she was able, with other women of means, to provide out of her own resources for Jesus and the disciples (Luke 8:3).

This group of women, to which Mary belonged, were exemplary disciples. They gave up their time to travel with Jesus as part of the entourage of disciples. They gave money to help Jesus preach the message about the Kingdom of God. They gave practical help to meet the ongoing needs of the group. And all of this was done from a deep sense of gratitude for what Jesus had done for them by healing them. For Mary it was a great privilege to be in the service of Jesus Christ.

LOYAL THROUGH ALL CIRCUMSTANCES

As one who followed Jesus in His travels, Mary would have experienced the highs and lows of His chequered ministry. There were times of success and moments of euphoria when the people acclaimed Him and jostled to hear Him. There were times of disappointment when even some of His own followers turned away and disowned Him and times when His enemies denounced Him. Mary remained constant in her discipleship and devotion to Christ.

We may safely guess that Mary's voice would have been raised in joyful acclamation when Jesus entered Jerusalem. This was a time of great rejoicing. Yet Mary was not far away when Jesus was in Pilate's Hall, or before Caiaphas, or when He was mocked by Herod's soldiers. Later, she was still following Jesus, but this time along the Via Dolorosa and up to Calvary. From His cross Jesus would see Mary not far away; sorrowful, concerned, caring, loyal to the end.

Here is loyalty of the highest order, a loyalty that challenges every reader of her story in the New Testament. Do we blow hot and cold in our loyalty? Do we remain constant in our loyalty to Christ through the highs and lows, successes and failures, advances and reverses, health and sickness that are part of the warp and woof of life for every one of us? It seems that Mary did. The story is told of an officer who approached Napoleon one day and asked him to honour a soldier who had shown outstanding bravery in a battle that had been fought not long before. 'And what,' asked the Emperor, 'did he do the next day?' In other words, was it a flash in the pan? Was he resting on his laurels? Was it simply one big effort or was it part of an ongoing service marked by bravery and loyalty?

Paul tells us that loyalty — he uses the word 'faithfulness' — is a fruit of the Spirit. The believers at Smyrna were told that if they would be faithful unto death the Lord would give them a crown of life (Rev. 2:10). Mary Magdalene is an outstanding example of faithfulness. In fact, Mary displayed greater consistency than many of the male disciples. For instance, Peter's loyalty had collapsed in the courtyard of the High Priest. Some of the other men had retreated into the anonymity of the throng in Jerusalem, but Mary remained near the cross, still unashamedly a disciple. With the example of Mary before us, who will dare describe women as the 'weaker vessel'?

THE FIRST WITNESS OF THE RESURRECTION
☐ On Mary was bestowed the unique privilege of being the first person to greet the risen Lord. Why was she chosen for this inestimable honour? There are at least two possible reasons.

First, Mary had stayed as close to Jesus as was humanly possible throughout the crucifixion and burial. She had been one of the women who had visited the tomb on the Friday evening. And, according to John, she was first at the tomb on the Sunday morning, lingering in the garden even when the other disciples, who had come to investigate the empty tomb, had gone away to 'their home'.

Mary had stayed as close as possible, in spite of the unbearable sadness she felt, a sadness beyond expression, and in spite of the painful mystery that troubled her mind as she would ask, again and again, 'Why did God allow Him to be killed?' The future was dark with foreboding. Yet, in spite of all these very negative factors she stayed as near as she could to Jesus. Then on that first Easter morning her devotion was vindicated and gloriously rewarded.

There are times when, like Mary, we are engulfed by anguish and mystery; times when our belief in a loving God seems to be contradicted by the things that happen to us. Mary's experience suggests that for those who stay close to Christ He will not only mark their loyalty but will vindicate their persevering faith.

Secondly, the other reason Jesus appeared first to Mary is that she loved Him with deep devotion. Hers was a love motivated by gratitude to the One who had saved her from the torment and despair of demon possession, the One who had given her a new life. Gratitude was a vital ingredient of her love for Jesus. We are often told, 'Christians should have a gratitude attitude'. Mary had a gratitude attitude. She challenges us to count our blessings and give thanks. It was Thomas à Kempis who said, 'Be thankful for the least gift, so shalt thou be meet to receive greater.'

Mary's love was a reverential love. We can safely jettison from our portrayal of Mary any speculation that her love for Jesus had a romantic or amorous dimension to it. It is totally unwarranted to think that Mary had a 'crush' on Jesus. Mary loved Jesus fervently, but it was the love of the disciple for her healer and teacher. This is borne out fully in the way she addresses Him on Easter morning as 'Rabboni' which means 'Teacher'.

☐ Mary became the first witness of the Resurrection. The word 'witness' has two meanings. It may simply mean that a person has witnessed an event, that is, observed it at first hand. It may also mean, however, that a person is called upon to give an account of what was observed. So that 'witness' covers both the 'seeing' and the 'telling'. Mary was a witness in both senses. She became the first to see the empty tomb and was the first to meet the risen Lord but then she was told by Jesus to go and announce the fact of the Resurrection to the other disciples. It is significant that a woman became the first herald to proclaim the Resurrection; the Resurrection which became a main theme of apostolic preaching.

Mary Magdalene is undoubtedly an important figure in the New Testament. Rescued from a tormented existence, she took full advantage of the new beginning which Jesus made possible for her. As a disciple, she built a new and creative life by devoting herself to serving Christ and His kingdom. Her qualities of an unwavering loyalty and a grateful love mark her out as an example to follow.

JAMES
The son of Zebedee
MARK 10:35-45; ACTS 12:1-3

The name James is the English form of the Hebrew and Greek name Jacob and appears to have been a very popular name in New Testament times. Two of the twelve apostles were called James and a brother of Jesus was also called James. It would have been an honourable name since one of the three great patriarchs of the early Hebrews was called Jacob. Popular and honourable the name might be, yet its literal meaning was 'one who takes by the heel', 'a supplanter'.

The James who is the subject of our study was the brother of John and the son of Zebedee. There is nothing in the gospels to indicate whether or not his father became a disciple. Beyond the fact that he was 'in the boat' when Jesus called his two sons and that he was prosperous enough to employ hired servants, nothing further is known about Zebedee.

Somewhat more is known about the mother of James. She is probably the Salome of the gospels. By comparing the references found in the gospels to the women who were present at the cross of Jesus, scholars have deduced that Salome was the mother of James and John, and that she was also the sister of Mary, the mother of Jesus. If this reasonable conjecture is correct, then James and John were cousins of Jesus. Salome was a committed disciple herself and belonged to a coterie of Galilean women who formed a kind of back-up group for Jesus and His disciples. She would be pleased and proud that her two sons were numbered among the twelve disciples, and we may take it for granted that they would have received motherly encouragement from her. In fact, the one blemish on her reputation is that she was over-ambitious for the advancement of her sons and made the precocious request for prominent positions for them in His kingdom. If she was

Jesus' aunt, she might have felt that the family ties would give her an advantage. Jesus never encouraged that idea.

From what we learn about James from the New Testament, we may note first of all:

THE CALL HE RECEIVED

James was one of the original four men summoned by Jesus to follow Him (Mark 1:16-20). What did that *call* involve for James?

☐ He was called to follow in a literal sense, to accompany Jesus through Galilee, Samaria and Judea. This meant for James, as for the others, leaving home and family. We do not know whether or not he was married, but since every Jewish male was expected to marry it is very likely that he had a wife. The call of Jesus meant that James would leave his occupation and, for long periods, it also meant leaving home and family to embark on the mission of the Messiah Jesus.

The call of Christ may still mean for some people moving out into a new role in the purpose of God, and this may mean leaving kith and kin to serve God in other parts of the world. In this way the Church has been planted in most of the countries of the world. For William Carey, following Christ meant travelling to India; for David Livingstone, it meant pioneering the way for the Gospel in central Africa; for Mother Teresa, following Christ led her to a ministry to the destitute of Calcutta. God still calls men and women to go to distant places to spread the Gospel and live it out in compassionate ministry among strangers in a foreign land.

Yet for the vast majority of Christians the call of Christ will not entail travelling to other parts of the world at all, but will rather involve them in being ambassadors for Christ where they already live and work. Those who go and those who stay share the same mission.

☐ James was called to follow not only in the literal sense but also in a spiritual, inward sense. Being a disciple meant more than simply being in a pupil-teacher relationship with Jesus.

To follow Christ involved a fuller commitment that included the heart's allegiance; it meant wholeheartedly embracing what He stood for; it meant following Him exclusively and no other; it meant espousing His cause as a willing promoter of that cause; it meant modelling his life on Christ. That is what following Christ implied for the first disciples, and there does not seem to be any reason for believing it should be any different for disciples today.

From the New Testament we may note further:

THE PRIVILEGE HE ENJOYED

With Peter and John, James formed an inner circle of three disciples who were especially close to Christ. These three were with Him on the Mount of Transfiguration (Matt. 17:1). They were the only disciples present at the raising of Jairus's daughter (Luke 8:51). They alone were invited to share in the destiny-laden prayers in Gethsemane (Mark 14:33). To be one of the three constituted an immense privilege, yet it was not a case of favours for favourites. They were being prepared for leadership.

It was a privilege to be on the Mount of Transfiguration but it also carried a responsibility, since they were given an insight into the glory of Christ and were directly told by God to listen to Jesus as the Son of God, and if Luke's account is followed then they heard a discussion about the death of Jesus in Jerusalem. All this involved responsibility. It was a privilege to be with Jesus in the Garden of Gethsemane, but they were there for a purpose and when they failed in that purpose they were gently rebuked.

If at any time James had imagined that because he was one of the 'inner' three he would be especially favoured and indulged, he would soon have been disabused of such a presumptuous notion. Jesus directed some of His strongest words of censure against these disciples. He rebuked James and John for their violent outburst against the Samaritan village. He told them, 'You do not know to what spirit you belong.' By their attitude, in other words, they were conducting themselves as if prompted by the devil.

As time went by, therefore, James, along with Peter and John, would realize that the honour of being close to Jesus was not just a matter of privilege; they were accountable for how they reacted to the privilege; the greater the privilege the greater the responsibility; 'to whom much is given much is expected'. Amos the prophet reminded Israel that their election as the people of God meant that they had to live like the people of God. To be a Christian is the greatest privilege, yet it carries the tremendous challenge to live and speak like a Christian. To be gifted is a great privilege, but it carried with it the obligation to use those gifts.

From the New Testament we learn in the third place:

THE FLAWS HE EXHIBITED

☐ He possessed an inflammable temper. Jesus nicknamed James and John 'the sons of thunder' (Mark 3:17). It seems that the two brothers shared this trait. We have clear evidence of this quick temper from an incident in the gospels. Jesus and His disciples were heading towards Jerusalem on one occasion and the most direct route took them through Samaria. However, the disciples who tried to arrange accommodation in the area were met with hostility from some Samaritans. When Jesus arrived at the scene, James and John were furious at the lack of respect shown by the Samaritans. 'Lord,' they blazed, 'shall we call fire down from heaven to consume them?' They were rebuked by Jesus: in this respect they seemed to have imbibed so little of His spirit as yet.

Uncontrolled anger can cause havoc. Only one letter separates anger from danger. The two words look alike and there is a close link between them in experience. Anger is dangerous and can destroy a relationship. In anger we act and speak less rationally then we might otherwise do. Someone said, 'Anger is a wind that blows out the lamp of the mind.'

There is a place for a passionate condemnation of the

wrongs and injustices which blight the lives of many people. That is a kind of righteous anger, and every responsible and sensitive person should be capable of strong feelings of that kind. It may be better, however, to call it by some other name since 'anger' suggests a negative and irrational state.

Anger can have a deleterious effect on health. John Hunter was an English physician, in the second half of the eighteenth century, who suffered from angina. He declared, 'My life is at the mercy of any scoundrel who chooses to put me in a passion.' This utterance proved prophetic: at a meeting of the board of St George's Hospital, London, of which he was a member, he became involved in a heated argument with other members. He walked out of the meeting, and dropped dead in the next room.

Jesus did not discard James and John because of their imperfections. His teaching and example would bring about changes in the lives of His disciples so that one day even members of the Jewish Sanhedrin would remark that these men had learned by being companions of Jesus (Acts 4:13). James was in the company of One who could help him resolve the problem of his unruly temper. James Denney, a renowned Scottish scholar and preacher whose writings are still respected today wrote, 'Who has not tried to overcome a fault, to work off a vicious temper, to break for good with an evil habit, or in some direction to sanctify himself, and withal to keep out of God's sight till the work is done? It is no use. Only the God of Peace can sanctify us.'

□ The second flaw to surface in the life of James was this: he was over-ambitious. As we have already noted, the brothers James and John were close to Jesus and may even have been his first cousins. It hardly reflects credit on them, therefore, if they were trying to exploit this advantage for yet further advantage. They asked Jesus, '"Let one of us sit at your right and the other at your left in your glory."' (Mark 10:37.)

William Barclay defended James and John for their ambition. He suggested that, given the apparent hopelessness of

Jesus' prospects in the face of growing official opposition, it showed a remarkable faith on their part to ask for prominent places in His future kingdom. This is an interesting slant on the story, but the reaction of the disciples, taken together with the comments of Jesus, make it altogether too kind a gloss on the ambition of the brothers.

This ambition on the part of James had three unfortunate ingredients: the pride that wanted power and glory; an absence of sensitivity towards the other disciples over whom James and John were trying to steal a march; the attempt to exploit a special relationship that may have been there with Jesus. James's attitude fell short of what was to become the Christian ideal as expressed by the apostle Paul. 'Do nothing out of selfish ambition or vain conceit, but in humility consider others better than yourselves.' (Phil 2:3.)

It is instructive to observe how patiently Jesus deals with the ambitious brothers. He tells them that all He can promise them is to share with Him in a costly obedience, but the privilege of sitting at His right or left will be given to those for whom that privilege has 'been prepared'. Jesus deals with them firmly yet patiently. He points out that true greatness consists in becoming a servant to others; serving others and not lording it over them. James and John are thus invited to learn from their mistake. They were disciples and the word disciple means 'learner'. A learner sometimes gets things wrong but learns from his or her mistakes. Failures can be woven into the fabric of our growth and progress if they are failures from which we gain valuable insights. A businessman had a sign on his desk which read: 'Please be patient with me; God has not finished with me yet.'

THE PRICE HE PAID

According to tradition, all the apostles of Christ died for the faith, but the martyrdom of James is the only one which is recorded in the New Testament. There is a touch of irony in the fact that he was the first to drink his Master's cup of death and be baptized with his Master's baptism of suffering. James had to make good his promise to drink that cup (Mark 10:35-40).

King Herod mounted an attack on the leaders of the Church. He took James, presumably because James was a known leader among the disciples. Herod probably thought that by his robbing the Church of its leaders the movement would wither and die. He was not the first or the last to adopt such a strategy. He had James summarily executed. When Herod saw how his action had pleased the Jewish leaders, he decided to give his popularity rating a further boost by seizing Peter. However, Peter escaped before Herod could put him through a token trial before putting him to death also.

Within the scope of a few verses, we read both of the fate that overtook James and the miraculous escape of Peter, an escape which Luke apparently linked to the Church's prayer and God's intervention (Acts 12:5). We are left to ponder why one apostle was allowed to die while the other escaped. We do not know the answer to these apparent contradictions; the perplexity remains; we see through a glass darkly as the apostle Paul tells us: we know in part. One apostle was called upon to die for his faith and the other was called to live for his faith.

A Roman coin was once found which bore the picture of an ox facing an altar and a plough. The words inscribed on it read: 'Ready for either'. The ox had to be ready for the dramatic and ultimate sacrifice of the altar or the long commitment of the plough. The Christian who dies a martyr's death and the Christian who lives a long life of faithful service are equally honourable servants of Christ.

Fifteen years after James and his brother John had left their nets on the shores of Galilee to follow Jesus, James became the first of the apostles to be faithful unto death.

PHILIP
The apostle
JOHN 1:43-46; 6:5; 12:21f; 14:8-11

Philip the apostle, not to be confused with Philip the evangelist, was one of the first disciples of Jesus. He hailed from Bethsaida, a fishing village on the shores of Galilee and, since Bethsaida was also the hometown of Simon and Andrew, he had probably known them for many years and maybe from childhood.

The first three gospels virtually ignore Philip, supplying his name as one of the disciples called by Jesus to be an apostle. In the gospel of John, however, the picture is very different and Philip figures in several incidents and, according to F. F. Bruce, was 'rescued from oblivion' by the fourth gospel.

From these references in John we may note five things about him:

THE FRIEND

The first thing Philip did after responding to the invitation to become a follower of Jesus was to go and find his friend Nathanael. Just as Andrew brought his brother Simon, so Philip persuaded Nathanael to meet Jesus. Nathanael was already a devout and sincere person without duplicity or affectation. Jesus acknowledged this quality of guilelessness in Nathanael and complimented him for it. '"Here is an Israelite worthy of the name; there is nothing false in him."' (John 1:47, NEB.) As far as a human being could be, he was transparently honest.

He was Philip's friend. Philip was a person who chose his friends with some care it seems. Friendship is one of the most potent influences for good or otherwise in our lives. An old saying warns: 'Choose your companions with care; you become what they are.'

Yet on this subject of friendship there does seem to be a

certain ambivalence, or so it seems, in the guidance given to us from the New Testament. On the one hand, the Christian is required to follow the example of Jesus and show a generous spirit of friendliness towards all people, regardless of colour, creed, or class. In fact, Jesus Himself was accused of consorting with sinners. He certainly mixed with all sorts of people. Christians are not greater than the Lord they serve and should be willing to extend the hand of friendship to all. Much emphasis is placed today on 'Friendship Evangelism', and statistical studies have established that more people come to faith in Christ through the friendship of Christians than through any other mode of outreach from the Church.

An openness to others in friendship, then, seems to be part of being a Christian. On the other hand, the New Testament makes it clear that to have the wrong kinds of friends is a danger to be avoided. The apostle Paul warned: 'Do not be misled: "Bad company corrupts good character."' (1 Cor. 15:33.) The Romans knew the damaging effects of wrong friendships and expressed the risks involved in a vivid metaphor, 'He who lies down with dogs will rise with fleas.' The apostle Paul counselled the Corinthians not to 'be unequally yoked with unbelievers'.

How are we to reconcile this friendly-to-all attitude with the caution not to cultivate wrong friendships? Maybe the example of Jesus will help resolve this dilemma. Jesus befriended all kinds of people without respect of persons in the course of a day's ministry but He also had a band of close friends whom He had chosen 'to be with' Him. A friendly attitude towards unbelievers may lead to creative friendships with people who may not share the faith, but Paul's warnings are important, and if a friendship is drawing a Christian away from Christ then that friendship may be costing too dear.

THE WITNESS

As soon as Philip had become a follower of Jesus, he began to talk about it to others. Where better to start than with his friend Nathanael! Now although Nathanael was a sincere kind of person he was also rather sceptical and it was not easy initially for Philip to get very far with him. Nathanael's scepticism was perfectly reasonable when we consider how far-fetched Philip's announcement must have seemed to him. Philip was asking him to believe that the Messiah, whose advent at some time in history Moses and the prophets had predicted centuries before, was in the neighbourhood, down the road! That took some believing, and Nathanael's reflexive dismissal of the idea was understandable. He was saying in effect, 'Are you honestly telling me that the Messiah, prom- ised centuries ago, has been growing up as our contemporary in Nazareth, a backwater if ever there was one, and if I take a few steps down the road I can meet Him? Come on, Philip. Get real!' Nathanael had a point.

Philip, however, was not easily put off, and he invited Nathanael to meet Jesus for himself so that he could make up his own mind. The result was quite remarkable. Upon meet- ing Nathanael, Jesus said that He had seen him sitting under a fig tree and described him as a true Israelite without guile. Nathanael took this as a manifestation of supernatural knowl- edge, which confirmed in his mind all that Philip had claimed for Jesus, and so Nathanael made his own confession, '"Rabbi, you are the Son of God; you are the king of Israel."' (John 1:49, NEB.) In using the phrase 'Son of God' Nathanael goes significantly further in his understanding of Jesus than is implied in the words of Philip.

Some scholars believe that Nathanael is the disciple who is called Bartholomew in the other three Gospels, and if this is correct then Philip was instrumental in bringing to Jesus one of the twelve apostles.

The way that Philip introduces Nathanael to Jesus is interesting for several reasons:

☐ His aim was simply to bring Nathanael to Jesus Christ. That is the aim of evangelism: to encourage others to meet with Jesus Christ and put their trust in Him as Saviour and

Lord of their lives. Philip wanted Nathanael to meet Jesus for himself and thus have first-hand knowledge of Him and not merely an opinion based on someone else's experience.

☐ Philip witnessed to someone he knew well. It is often quite difficult for Christians to speak about their faith to the people who are close to them. Greater sensitivity and tact are often needed to speak about Christ to our own families, if they do not share the faith, than to people we know less well. Yet sensitive witness by Christians to their families and friends remains one of the most fruitful forms of evangelism.

☐ The way that Philip introduced Nathanael to Jesus is also an example of gentle persistence. He did not give up at the first rebuff from Nathanael. He tried another approach. He did not argue with Nathanael; instead, he simply said, 'Come and see.' It worked.

THE PRACTICALLY-MINDED

The next time Philip is mentioned in John is in the story of the feeding of the five thousand. On that occasion, Jesus was concerned that the crowds were hungry. He turned to Philip and asked where they could buy bread to feed the people. Why did he single out Philip? The most likely explanation is that Jesus turned to the most practically-minded of the disciples, the person with the best grasp of what might need to be done to solve the situation that had arisen. This view of Philip is confirmed when we read on in the story and discover that he has already estimated how much money would be needed to provide a small snack for every person in the crowd. Philip realized, however, that even if there had been enough bread in the surrounding villages the modest resources of the disciples, which might have been the two hundred denarii mentioned by Philip, would not begin to meet the needs of such a number of people. But at least Philip had already tried to figure out the size of the problem. This suggests he was the kind of person who applied his mind to practical details. Had there been a way to meet the need from available resources, Philip would have thought of it. There is always need for Christians who are practically-minded. Someone once said, 'He who would love another must do so in minute particulars.'

In his book *How Come, God?* David Howard tells of a young couple living abroad who lost a 2-year-old child in tragic circumstances. The distraught husband needed help to arrange to take the body of his child, his inconsolable wife, and what belongings they had out of the country as soon as possible. A missionary offered encouragement: 'Just trust the Lord. Just rest in His strong arms and it'll be all right.' Then he walked away. The words seemed hollow and irrelevant.

It was William Purcell who said, 'The service of God, like a coin, has two sides: Mary's as well as Martha's: Martha's as well as Mary's; the worshipping and meditative as well as the active.'

THE INTERMEDIARY

The next time we hear of Philip is towards the end of Jesus' life when they are in Jerusalem (John 12:20-22). Certain Greeks had come to Jerusalem and, having heard reports of the ministry of Jesus, they were eager to meet Him. These Greeks who had come 'for the feast' were probably 'God-fearers', that is, uncircumcised adherents of Judaism, who had forsaken the polytheistic religion of Greece and worshipped, instead, the one God, the God of Israel.

They approached the disciples and appear to have singled out Philip and said to him, 'Sir, we would see Jesus.' They were really asking Philip to introduce them to Jesus. Why did they ask Philip? A possible explanation is that he had a Greek name. He and Andrew were the only members of the twelve to have Greek names when Jesus called them. (Philip means 'lover of horses'.) Maybe the Greeks had overheard someone refer to Philip by name and because it was a Greek name they felt some affinity with him, just as an Englishman aboard might feel an affinity with someone called Smith.

If this guess is correct, then Philip's name became a point of contact with the Greeks. A point of contact or affinity is often an important factor in Christian witness and it could be almost anything a believer has in common with a non-believer. The point of affinity could be a hobby, an interest, an occupation, the rearing of children, similar experiences, similar backgrounds, common problems, and so on. We see Jesus using a point of contact with the woman at the well. In many ways, Jesus and the woman were worlds apart, but they had one thing in common: the need for water to drink. That shared need became the starting point of a conversation which would lead eventually to the Samaritan woman's confessing Jesus to be the Messiah.

When the Greeks requested Philip to take them to Jesus, he seems to have been in some doubt as to whether or not it was permissible to bring a group of Greeks to the Master. He conferred with Andrew and together they took the request to Jesus. One commentator accuses Philip of ducking the decision, and describes Philip's caution as passing on the responsibility. This is an entirely harsh and unnecessary indictment of Philip. He did not try to put the Greeks off, nor did he delay taking action. He simply thought it wise to consult Andrew, and that is surely indicative not of indecisiveness, but of modesty and caution.

THE THEOLOGIAN

The last time we meet Philip in the gospels is in the Upper Room. Jesus was teaching His disciples. In particular He was preparing them for His death which He knew to be imminent. For their part, the disciples found this talk about His death disturbing, unsettling and unwelcome. How could they face life without Jesus when for three years everything had centred in Him? Jesus tried to reassure them and put their minds at rest by pointing out that His parting from them was part of God's good purpose. Going before them to Heaven He would prepare a place for them. He comforted them by speaking of His death as a going home to the Father's house. It was as He spoke these words that Philip interrupted Him. '"Lord,"' he said, '"show us the Father and that will be enough for us."' (John 14:8-11.)

In putting this question, Philip was not speaking as an agnostic asking for rational proof of God's existence. As a Jew and as a follower of Jesus he would already be a believer in God. What Philip wanted was more knowledge about the God in whom they already believed.

The reply given to Philip was an amazing statement. Jesus said, '"Anyone who has seen me has seen the Father."' Staggering though this claim must have seemed, the disciples believed it, and it became a conviction deeply held by the apostolic preachers of the Gospel and a fundamental tenet of the doctrine they taught. The writer to the Hebrews, for example, expresses lyrically the claim of Jesus: 'the son who is the effulgence of God's splendour and the stamp of God's very being'. (Heb. 1:3, NEB.) In theological terms, we see the words of Jesus to Philip as confirmation of the Christian view that Jesus Christ is God the Son. In practical terms the claim made by Jesus may mean three things:

The teaching of Jesus conveyed the mind of God.

The life lived by Jesus reflected the character of God.

The deeds of Jesus revealed the purpose of God.

We are indebted to Philip for putting the question to Jesus, for without the question there would have been no answer.

This brings us to the end of our look at the references to Philip in the New Testament. There are a number of stories about Philip's later life, but the magical and fantastical elements in these traditions betray their legendary character. Eusebius, the Bishop of Caesarea and known as the 'Father of Church history', tells us that Philip had a very fruitful ministry in Asia Minor and that he was martyred at Hierapolis. Visitors to the ancient site of Hierapolis are shown what is believed to be the tomb of Philip.

Whatever may be the truth about Philip's later life, it is

as we see him through John's gospel that we best remember him. He is the disciple who witnessed to his friend; he is the disciple who was practically-minded; he is the disciple with whom the Greeks had a point of contact; and he is the disciple who asked questions about the Father.

THOMAS
The patron saint of doubters
JOHN 20:24-29

The way that Thomas is always described as 'doubting Thomas' is unfair to the apostle Thomas on two counts. In the first place, it implied that he was prone to doubt as someone who was temperamentally predisposed to it. There is no reason to suggest that this was the case. It is unfair in the second place because it suggested that this is the main characteristic for which Thomas should be remembered.

On the evidence of John's gospel, it would be just as correct to call him 'courageous Thomas'. We can check the evidence for this. When Jesus began to make a move to go to Bethany at the time of Lazarus' death, the disciples were very apprehensive and did their best to dissuade Him. They knew that, given the opposition Jesus had already encountered from Jewish officialdom, to go south into Judea would be to court disaster. They wanted Jesus to stay in the north where most of His support was centred, and keep well away from the area where danger loomed. At that moment, Thomas went out on a limb and took a different attitude from the others. He said, '"Let us also go, that we may die with him."' (John 11:16.) That bold statement by Thomas must have been of real encouragement to Jesus, as he took the momentous decision to go first to Bethany and then to Jerusalem. That deep devotion to Christ was as much a part of the story of Thomas as the transient doubt for which he is better known. Yet we call him 'doubting Thomas' and not 'courageous Thomas'.

Even the story in John that recounts the doubt of Thomas relates the most remarkable confession of faith made by the apostle. Once he was truly convinced that Jesus had risen from the dead, he said, '"My Lord and my God!"' This was a confession of faith that went beyond a belief in the Resurrection. It was an affirmation of faith in the divine status of

Christ. Yet we go on calling him 'doubting Thomas' and not 'believing Thomas'. Why do we remember his doubt and not his courage or his faith? Maybe there is something we need to learn about the way we think of others. When someone fails in some way, that failure tends to loom large in our view of that person; it colours our thinking. Are we willing to take into account the fact that the lapse might have been an isolated incident? Are we ready to remember all the good and positive things about the person?

All that being said, however, we must admit that, although it is quite unfair to label Thomas as a doubter, it was his experience of doubt and the way that Jesus helped him through that doubt that has given Thomas a unique place in the thinking of Christians. We might almost say that he is the patron saint of doubters, and many who have passed through the valley of doubt and uncertainty have found reassurance in the example of Thomas.

In reviewing this doubt of Thomas we may note, in the first place, that

IT WAS NOT BORN OF A REBELLIOUS SPIRIT

There is a certain genus of doubt which arises out of a deliberate intention not to believe. A person may have reasons for not wanting to believe in God. It may be that he or she may wish to be totally autonomous, a free spirit without having to account to a Sovereign God. There may be many other reasons for not wanting to believe in God. There was nothing of this kind of hidden rebellion in the doubt of Thomas. He would have probably given anything to know with certainty that what the other disciples were excitedly proclaiming was true. He longed for it to be true. It was surely because the other disciples knew that the doubt Thomas was experiencing was not an expression of disloyalty to Jesus, but something that was painful and disturbing to him, that prompted them to encourage him to stay with them in spite of his rather outrageous demand.

The doubter should be surrounded with sensitive support rather than with criticism and disappointment. Just as doubt was part of the experience of an apostle so it can spring up in the heart of the most ardent believer. Some writers believe that doubt is an inevitable part of the Christian's experience. 'Faith without doubt is dead', is their view. F. Buechner put the same thought in somewhat less biblical language when he wrote, 'Doubts are the ants in the pants of faith. They keep us alive and moving.' A theological student went to his professor and complained that while he had to wrestle with doubts the professor seemed to speak always with assurance about his faith. The Professor replied, 'Young man, I have doubts you haven't even thought of.' Thomas's doubt does not set him apart as different or exceptional. It is because doubt is so much a part of our common experience that readers of the gospel can readily identify with Thomas.

In considering this doubt of Thomas we may note, in the second place, that so far as Thomas was concerned

IT WAS A REASONABLE DOUBT

All the talk of Jesus' rising from the dead and passing through bolted doors was too fantastical for him to accept. Doubt seemed the most rational response.

There are many people who have a similar difficulty with the Resurrection. It is something that is quite outside their experience. All the people known to them who have died have stayed dead. To doubt the Resurrection seems to them, therefore, the most sensible response. In fact, however, it may not be the most rational or scientific attitude to say, 'I will believe what I can observe; and that only will I believe.' The more scientific approach seems to be to say, 'I will look at all the evidence and come to a conclusion on the basis of all the evidence.' When we think of the Resurrection, then, the scientific approach will take into account all the facts.

There are many evidences for the Resurrection. There is the witness of many ordinary people, down-to-earth kinds of people, trustworthy men and women. They were not mystics given to visions; they were not dreamers given to flights of fantasy. They were people just like Thomas who needed to be convinced, telling the things they had seen and heard, a unanimous testimony. Another piece of evidence for the Resurrection is the birth, growth and spread of the Church throughout the world. Without the Resurrection there would have been no Church or New Testament. A rational approach to the Resurrection will take into account all the evidence.

In considering this doubt of Thomas we may note, in the third place, that he doubted because

HE FAILED TO BELIEVE WHAT JESUS HAD PREDICTED

Several times during His ministry, Jesus had spoken about His death and resurrection. For example, He compared His time in the tomb with the three days Jonah was inside the great fish (Matt. 12:40). Then again, when He came down the Mount of Transfiguration He told the disciples to keep quiet about the things they had witnessed 'until the Son of Man had risen from the dead'. (Mark 9:9.) Now this raises a difficulty for students of the New Testament. If Jesus had so clearly predicted that He would rise again from the dead, why were the disciples taken by surprise when it actually happened? Some scholars say that these sayings in the gospels are *vaticinia ex eventu*, that is, prophecies after the event. This means that where we find references to the resurrection before the crucifixion we must attribute those sayings to the early Church and not to Jesus Himself. There are formidable objections to this way of understanding the New Testament. When we do this kind of thing, we are really setting ourselves up as arbiters who decide subjectively what is to be attributed to Jesus and what is to be attributed to the early Church. It also means that we accept that the gospel writers were guilty of deception, placing on the lips of Jesus words they knew He had never uttered.

But if we accept that, before His death, Jesus did speak of His Resurrection, how do we explain the surprise of the disciples when it happened?

☐ It may well be the case that they were confused as to what Jesus meant when He spoke about the Resurrection. We know, for instance, that Martha found it confusing when Jesus spoke about resurrection at the tomb of Lazarus. Her thoughts went immediately to a resurrection at the last day (John 11:24). It was not something she expected could happen in her lifetime.

We may also recall the puzzlement of the three disciples, as they came down from the Mount of Transfiguration, trying to figure out what Jesus meant when He said that the Son of Man would rise from the dead (Mark 9:9). They had no single, agreed view of what Jesus was trying to tell them. They might have interpreted Jesus' words as having a symbolic meaning, and if that were the case then they would not be expecting a literal resurrection.

☐ There may be another reason why the Resurrection took them by surprise. When Jesus spoke about His imminent death most of the disciples appear to have resisted the idea. It was something they did not want to think about; it would be for them the ultimate tragedy. It has been said that we hear what we want to hear and shut the rest out. To think of life without Jesus was something quite unimaginable. They did not hear what He was saying about the Resurrection because they were not even listening to what He was saying about His death. Thomas, then, would not believe in the Resurrection because He had not listened to what Jesus Himself had predicted, but this was something he had in common with the other disciples.

The story of Thomas and his doubt is a source of encouragement to all who experience doubts. It is encouraging in two particular ways:

First, it encourages us to believe that Jesus Christ draws near to the sincere doubter. Jesus made a special appearance for the sake of Thomas. Nor is there anything in what Jesus said to Thomas to suggest that by doubting, or by expressing his doubt, Thomas had sinned. Jesus did not condemn Thomas. He drew near to reassure him. When we pass through dark times of doubt we may be sure that doubt does not constitute a sin nor will we incur the displeasure of God. Jesus drew near to the sincere doubter.

Secondly, the story of Thomas encourages us to continue to meet in fellowship and worship with other Christians when we are experiencing doubts. Thomas, though absent on the first occasion when Jesus appeared in the upper room, was not absent on the next occasion. He kept himself firmly within the company of the disciples. This proved to be a wise decision. If his doubts were to be resolved at all, the most likely place for that to happen would be among the disciples. When troubled by doubts, we do not help resolve those doubts by retreating into isolation and cutting ourselves off from the people of faith. Jesus met Thomas and helped him through his doubt when he was among the disciples in the upper room. Jesus still meets us and speaks to us when we meet with others in His name. That is His promise.

A final word. While it is true, as we have seen, that Jesus did not condemn Thomas for his doubt, neither did He commend him for it. His doubt was not a vice but neither was it a virtue. It is quite fashionable to regard doubt as intellectually superior to faith. There is nothing of this in the story of Thomas. In fact, Jesus praises not Thomas but those who believe without demanding visible proof. Doubt is not superior to faith, but the believer will never be wholly free of doubts, even when he is walking by faith. The story of Thomas is important to every Christian pilgrim who struggles with doubt.

JUDAS
So near, yet so far
MARK 14:44-46

To be called a 'Judas' is to suffer the ultimate insult. For two thousand years the name Judas has had a sinister ring for people who have embraced the Christian faith. Yet before Judas Iscariot betrayed Christ, the name had been an honourable one in Jewish history. According to Genesis (29:35), the name means 'praise' or 'praise the Lord'. One scholar elaborates upon the meaning of the word: 'As the name of the tribe of Judah, which honoured Judah, the fourth son of Jacob, as its ancestor, the proper name Judas served in the early postexilic period to emphasize the purity of descent. In a later period, as Israel's past came to be placed in an ideal light, one wished the child with this name something of the glory of previous times.' (M. Limbeck, *Exegetical Dictionary of the New Testament*, page 197.) The name would also be celebrated in Jesus' time as the name of the national hero Judas Maccabaeus who, just over a hundred years before Christ, against all odds, had thwarted the colonizing ambitions of the Seleucid king Antiochus.

In Christian history, however, the name has been a synonym for treachery. Judas betrayed his master and friend, the greatest Person he had ever known. It would be unthinkable for Christian parents to give a baby boy the name Judas!

There are those who have read the story of Judas' betrayal and found it difficult to believe that someone so close to Christ could be capable of such treachery. They have offered alternative explanations to account for what he did; explanations which portray Judas as misguided rather than malicious; explanations which show him in a kinder light, attributing to him motives very different from the greed and callous opportunism usually associated with the betrayal. There are at least three such theories.

□ One theory depicts Judas as a passionate patriot who had come to the conclusion that Jesus was not interested in the liberation of the land from foreign domination. Jesus was too friendly towards foreigners and even Romans. By betraying Jesus, Judas was acting out of love for his country. He was prepared to sacrifice Jesus for the cause. There is no evidence for such a view of Judas.

□ Then there is the theory that Judas might have been a loyal but impatient disciple. He believed that Jesus had the power miraculously to extricate Himself from any situation. In this view, the purpose of the betrayal was to force Jesus into a confrontation with the Jewish authorities and thus compel Him to display His Messianic power and maybe establish His claim to rule.

□ A variant of this latter view depicts Judas as disappointed with what he perceived to be the delaying tactics of Jesus. Palm Sunday had seen a groundswell of popular support for Jesus, but instead of capitalizing on that support and allowing the momentum of Palm Sunday to carry Him to power Jesus temporized and 'went to ground' in Bethany. Judas decided to take matters into his own hands. By bringing the arresting party to Gethsemane, Judas would force Jesus to end the procrastination and display His power by subduing His enemies. It follows from this theory that although Judas might have been wrongheaded, his heart was in the right place. His only intention was to trigger a response on the part of Jesus that would lead Him to take His place as King of Israel.

It may be that these attempts to portray Judas in a more favourable light are no more than 'the fruit of a desire in preachers to say something new rather than something true'. Indeed, the New Testament leaves little or no room for such imaginary reconstructions. John says of Judas, 'he was a thief' (John 12:6); Luke says that Satan 'entered into' Judas (Luke 22:3); Jesus said of him, '"It would be better for him if he had not been born."' (Matt. 26:24.) And elsewhere Jesus said, 'Have I chosen twelve and one of you is a devil?'

The one fact that could be construed as offering some support for these more 'lenient' views of Judas' motives is that when Judas realized that Jesus was being placed on trial for His life he went and hanged himself. If Judas had expected Jesus to be arrested and tried, why was he so upset when it happened? At least it shows that he was not totally cynical nor wholly driven by greed. In any case, it is not for us to judge Judas. Let that person who has never betrayed Christ, in one form or another, cast the first stone. What we can do, however, is to learn from what went wrong in Judas' life.

PREOCCUPIED WITH MONEY

It appears that, from the beginning of Jesus' ministry, Judas had taken a keen interest in the finances of the group and had obviously been allowed to take charge of what probably was a small reserve of money which was necessary to provide essential supplies. It is likely that, contrary to suggestion, the reserve was not to facilitate the payment of synagogue taxes, since Jesus told the disciples they were 'exempt'. (Matt. 17:26.) However, there was more than a whiff of suspicion that Judas was helping himself from the bag. We learn this from the passage in the fourth gospel where Judas voices his protest against what he considered to be the wasteful extravagance of Mary's gesture in anointing Jesus with a very expensive perfumed ointment. He complained that the ointment could have been sold, if Mary had only handed it over, presumably to him, and would have realized thirty pounds (300 denarii) which could have been given to the poor. John believed, however that this concern for the poor was a simulated sympathy with an ulterior motive. 'He said this, not out of any concern for the poor, but because he was a thief; he had charge of the common purse, and used to pilfer money kept in it.' (John 12:6, REB.) However small the sums of money involved, the treasurer had turned embezzler.

All the warnings Judas had heard from Jesus about the dangers of wealth had fallen on deaf ears. Judas had the best teacher the world has seen, yet he failed to profit by that teaching. Money was his master.

As the days of Holy Week came and passed, Judas became more restive. It is possible that he saw more clearly than the other disciples which way the wind was blowing, and he realized how things were likely to end. He knew that Caiaphas would finally catch up with Jesus and that He would be arrested, and that might be the end of the whole Messianic enterprise. Did Judas at that point conceive his plan to salvage some advantage for himself from the situation? After all, he would have to consider his own future and a little money would certainly help. And so was born the plan to betray Jesus. He would not come out of all of this empty-handed, thirty pieces of silver would be some resource with which to face the uncertain days ahead. However, as he went away and the enormity of the treachery he had perpetrated dawned on his mind, he found that he could not face the future or live with himself, and he committed suicide.

What happened to Judas is a warning to all who are tempted to allow money and its acquisition to become the be-all and end-all of life. The example of Judas illustrates how powerfully the desire for money can take control of a person's mind and heart. In September of 1995, a young Brazilian in Sao Paulo won a million dollars on a lottery but could not find the ticket. He was convinced that his girlfriend had lost it, and he became so incensed that he took a gun and shot her dead. Hernando deSerra told reporters, 'When I couldn't find that ticket, I was so sure Francesca had lost it; I went crazy. To have so much money and then lose it because of somebody else's stupidity is enough to drive anybody to murder.' He later found the ticket in his own shirt pocket. The thought of owning such a large sum of money swept his self-control away and disturbed his equilibrium, robbing him of a proper sense of values. That is an extreme example, but it dramatically demonstrated the power of the love of money which, according to the Bible, is the root of all evil. Of course, everyone needs money to live and poverty is not a virtue *per se*. But, like fire, money is a good servant but a bad master. It has been said, 'Money cannot buy one necessity of the soul.'

The sad irony in Judas' case is that he had probably been appointed to be treasurer in the beginning because he knew best how to manage money. He had a specific role and that was something the other disciples did not have. He had a real opportunity to serve his Master and the others, yet he attempted to use his gift for personal gain. As Herbert Lockyer wrote, ' . . . he prostituted his gift. His very endowment became a snare. A blessing was turned into a curse.'

FAILED TO BELIEVE IN THE FORGIVENESS OF GOD

That Judas committed suicide suggests that he was convinced God could not forgive him. He probably regarded his treacherous betrayal as an unpardonable evil. A certain reading of the New Testament might suggest that Judas was predestined to play the part of the betrayer. In John (17:12, KJV) Jesus calls Judas 'the son of perdition', and in Acts chapter one, when Judas is replaced as an apostle, his death is described as going 'to his own place' (1:25, KJV). This may give the impression that Judas was fated to damnation. But as one scholar points out, 'The Lord's foreknowledge of him does not imply fore-ordination that Judas must inexorably become the traitor.' (Raph P. Martin, *The Illustrated Bible Dictionary*, Vol. 2, IVP, page 831.) Nor should we conclude that forgiveness was not possible for Judas. No limit should be placed on the power of God's mercy and grace, even for a Judas.

There can be no doubt that Judas experienced a burning sense of remorse, a desolating sense of self-loathing, when he realized what he had done. What was Judas trying to say when he returned the money to the High Priest? Was he hoping it might lead to the release of Jesus? But he must have known that his pathetic gesture would cut no ice with the High Priest. Was he trying to say that his betrayal did not mean that he had switched sides and had turned state's evidence to safeguard himself? By returning the money, Judas was probably expressing his deep feelings of remorse. Remorse, however, on its own without true repentance is a cul-de-sac, a dead end; remorse is full of despair, self-despising and foreboding and is devoid of any sense of hope. There is a difference between remorse and repentance. Remorse is really obsessive regret: repentance also has the component of regret, but it sees beyond regret to the new beginning which God gives to all who genuinely repent. Remorse is fixated on the past; repentance includes a sorrow for the sin of the past but, accepting the forgiveness of God, looks forward to change and amendment of life. Remorse is negative; repentance is positive. The difference between the experience of Judas and Peter illustrates the difference between remorse and repentance. They were both disloyal to Jesus, but Peter believed that he might have an opportunity to express his sorrow to Jesus and find forgiveness. Peter found that forgiveness and went on to become a great leader in the Church, whereas Judas ended his life in ignominious death.

It is clear that the other disciples regarded Judas as having been a fellow apostle. He had been called by Jesus just as they had been called and he had shared 'the ministry and apostleship' (Acts 1:25, KJV). They do not suggest that he had been a charlatan all the way along. By his 'transgression' he had forfeited his place and become apostate. Here is the tragedy of Judas. He had been present to witness many notable miracles. He had heard the teaching of Jesus, both the public discourses and the private tuition given to the disciples. His example stands as a warning to all who follow Christ not to be complacent or allow worldly concerns and the cares of this life to choke the seed of God's Word.

JOHN MARK

The disciple who made a great come-back

2 TIMOTHY 4:11

A teacher once held up a sheet of paper before her class. In the middle of the sheet there was a black spot. She asked her class to tell her what they could see. 'A black spot!' they chorused. They were actually looking at a large white sheet, yet it was the spot that caught their attention.

When we think of the New Testament character known as John Mark, there is a good chance that it is his 'black spot' that will come to mind. We remember how he deserted Paul and Barnabas at a critical stage in the first missionary itinerary outreach into Asia Minor. It is unfair, of course, to remember Mark for that one lapse, but the incident does stand out since there is little else by way of biographical data available on the life of Mark. Nevertheless, what we do know about him is worth noting.

HE PROFITED FROM HIS EARLY ADVANTAGES

As a young man, Mark enjoyed many advantages of both a spiritual and material kind. His mother Mary appears to have been a woman of wealth and status, as well as being a Christian. Their home in Jerusalem was of a size that could conveniently serve as a meeting-place for Christians. They probably had domestic staff, one of whom was a maidservant called Rhoda. Mark's cousin Barnabas was a wealthy landowner (Acts 4:36, 37). If we put all these facts together, they show that Mark's family was well off. Two factors tend to support the conjecture that Mark's father was dead by the time Mark was involved in Christian witness: there is no reference to his father and their home is called 'Mary's'.

Mark was surrounded by people who were inspiring examples of Christian faith and service. Mary's home was a place where Christ was truly honoured, where prayer was as natural as conversation, and where Christians came to seek and find fellowship and mutual encouragement. His cousin Barnabas was an outstanding Christian of whom it was later said, ' . . . a good man, full of the Holy Spirit and of faith' (Acts 11:24). Then there was Peter. We know that in the writing of his gospel, Mark drew on Peter's preaching. And when the apostle was released from prison he went straight to Mark's home, and all this suggests a close bond with Peter. As a young man, therefore, Mark had a godly mother, a Christian home, and the influence of Barnabas and Peter.

Such advantages were obviously not wasted on Mark. He became a disciple and began to involve himself in the work of the Kingdom. How pleased Mary must have been to see her son progress in discipleship. William Temple wrote, 'The most influential of all educational factors is the conversation in a child's home.' Of course, there can be no guarantees that a child will follow a good example, and sometimes children choose to go down the wrong path. Yet many are influenced by their parents. Francis Quarles, three-and-a-half centuries ago, wrote, 'In early life I had nearly been betrayed into the principles of infidelity; but there was one argument in favour of Christianity which I could not refute, and that was the consistent character of my own father.' John Mark was also numbered among those who, given the best example, responded to it to his own spiritual profit.

The second thing that stands out in the life of Mark is this:

HE LEARNED FROM HIS MISTAKES

We come now to that 'black spot' in the ministerial career of Mark. On the first missionary tour from Antioch, Paul and Barnabas took Mark with them as a helper. The Greek word used by Luke to describe this help is variously translated as 'attendant', 'helper', and 'servant'. We must not be misled by these translations, however, into thinking that Mark was nothing more than an errand boy or a porter to carry their bags.

He was very much part of the team. In fact, the Greek word rendered 'helper' (*huperetes*) is used in Luke (1:2) in the sense of 'minister of the Word'.

One scholar speculated that with Mark's special knowledge of the life of Jesus he was well placed to serve as a catechist for new converts. If this suggestion is correct and John Mark was fulfilling a vital teaching role, then it would explain why Paul felt so bitterly disappointed when the young Mark decided to quit after they had completed only the first phase of their itinerary. But quit he did and returned to Jerusalem.

Why did Mark turn tail and abandon the other two?

☐ Was it fear of moving into an unknown area with all the accompanying dangers? They were moving, at that point, into a new continent (modern Turkey) which might have been unfamiliar to Mark.

☐ Or was it nothing more than plain homesickness? The nineteenth-century scientist, Professor T. H. Huxley, once wrote about coming home to England after a considerable stay on the continent of Europe. He said, 'I reached Folkestone on a rainy day. The streets of that little southern town were thick with mud, but I could have lain down and rolled in it; I was so glad that it was English mud!' The thought of home can exert a powerful pull on the heart.

☐ Perhaps he resented the fact that Paul was more and more assuming the leadership role and had already become the principal spokesman of the group. Mark might have thought that his cousin Barnabas had the stronger claim to be in charge, especially in view of his original commission from the Jerusalem church.

☐ Perhaps Mark was uncomfortable with the alacrity with which Paul was turning to the Gentiles in his ministry with an increasing tendency to use his Roman name — Paul. Well, these are all guesses and we cannot be sure what caused Mark to return home to Jerusalem since no explanation is offered by Luke to account for his decision. The fact that he weakened in his resolve is another reminder that Bible characters were 'bone of our bone'; they knew, as we know, what it means to be fearful; they knew, as we know, what it means to feel that the pressures of life are more than we can take.

Mark's desertion was something Paul found difficult to understand or forgive, and when, some time later, they were back in Antioch and it was mooted that a second missionary journey be undertaken and Barnabas wanted to take Mark with them Paul adamantly refused. Barnabas was convinced that they should take Mark, but Paul stood his ground and would not yield. This resulted in a rift between the two missionaries: Barnabas took Mark and sailed again to Cyprus; Paul took Silas and went in a different direction.

Mark must have struggled with a welter of emotions as he set off with Barnabas. It must have been disturbing to realize that he had been responsible for triggering an altercation between two of the greatest men in the Church. He was resolved, no doubt, to last the course this time, but may even have had nagging doubts about that. He certainly did not want to let the Lord down again, or Barnabas for that matter. How would Mark cope with the emotional turmoil he must have experienced? From his subsequent success as a minister and writer of a Gospel and from the way he was fully reinstated in the good esteem of the apostle Paul, we can safely conclude that he must have handled the inner conflict in a positive way.

One interesting possibility is that Mark learned from both the severity of Paul and the gentleness of Barnabas. Paul held a mirror up to Mark and forced him to realize that broken promises, half-finished tasks, missed opportunities, desertion of his post, all added up to a serious breach of loyalty on his part, not only to the two apostles but also to God. Mark had discouraged his colleagues at a critical moment, a moment when they needed encouragement. Paul could not easily forget, and obviously felt that it was too soon to be trusting Mark again.

Now Mark could have reacted to the uncompromising

harshness of Paul's inflexible attitude by vowing never to have anything to do with him again. He could have regarded Paul's stance as punitive and without compassion. Yet there is every reason to believe that, although he might have been hurt by Paul's severity, he responded to the criticism in a positive way. He learned from his mistake and put it behind him. A positive response meant telling himself that Paul was not acting with a vindictive spirit but was saying something Mark needed to hear and take on board. What evidence is there that Mark took the criticism resiliently? The next we hear of him is about ten years later. He is with Paul in Rome and joining with the apostle in sending greetings to the Colossian church (Col. 4:10). Paul asks the church at Colossae to welcome Mark into their fellowship. Why should that be necessary? Well, it sometimes takes a long time to live down mistakes and if Paul's disagreement with Barnabas was well known, then it may be that even all those years later it was necessary for Paul to commend Mark warmly as a close friend so as to assure the Colossians that he was entirely worthy of their goodwill. Clearly by this time Mark and Paul were on the best possible terms. Mark had taken the criticism and learned from it. Later still Paul speaks appreciatively of Mark: 'Get Mark and bring him with you, because he is helpful to me in my ministry.' (2 Tim. 4:11.)

If this assumption is right and Mark took the criticism of Paul and benefited from it, it provides us with an example to follow whenever we have to face up to criticism. Do we respond as positively to criticism as he did? Are we able to say, 'Faithful are the wounds of a friend'? Dr David Read has well expressed the best way to respond to criticism: 'If we allow the hurt to infuriate us into an explosion of self-justification or if we retire into a shell to wallow in a sense of grievance, then we are bearing the wound in the "world's way", and our soul begins to shrivel. If, in spite of the pain, we are humble enough to ask God to show us where we have gone wrong, courageous enough to admit our fault and trusting enough to accept the transforming power of Christ, then we are bearing the wound in God's way . . . and our soul begins to expand.'

It seems, then, that Mark responded positively to Paul's criticism and probably learned from it. Yet Mark inevitably would have been affected by Paul's stance and it would almost certainly have left him feeling dispirited and dejected. He needed someone like the gentle Barnabas to come along and tell him to stand tall, dust himself down and start all over again. By his attitude, Barnabas was telling Mark that he was not being rejected by God. Barnabas had obviously forgiven Mark and held out to him the opportunity of another beginning, an opportunity which the younger man took with both hands. If Paul dealt him a blow, Barnabas bound up the wound; if Paul taught him to weigh carefully the full measure of his failure, Barnabas taught him that God is gracious and no failure is final for those who will begin again. For Mark to be able to make a proper and balanced response to his own failure, he needed to hear what both Paul and Barnabas were saying.

The third and final observation about Mark takes us outside the New Testament sources.

HE TRIUMPHED OVER LIMITATIONS

There are good reasons for believing Mark was known to many by a nickname, and a rather unflattering nickname at that. A reference to this nickname occurs in a prologue to his gospel, dating from the second century. In Greek this name was *kolobdaktulos*, which may be rendered as 'stumpyfingered'. This may mean simply that he had naturally short fingers, but if the stumpiness was as obvious as to earn for him a nickname, then it is more likely that one or both of his hands were deformed. At least there was some peculiarity about his hands.

Dr E. M. Blaiklock made an imaginative guess as to how he became manually maimed. He accepts the widely-supported view that Mark was the unnamed 'young man' clad only in a linen sheet in the Garden of Gethsemane on the night Jesus was betrayed and arrested (Mark 14:51, 52). When the armed group came from the High Priest to apprehend Jesus, they seized Mark. Leaving his linen covering in their hands, he slipped from their grasp and ran away, perhaps, speculates Dr Blaiklock, 'with a mutilating swordslash across his fingers'. Whether this ingenious suggestion is correct or not, there was something unusual about his hands.

Is it not remarkable that the first gospel to be penned was written by old 'Stumpyfingers', that is to say, by a man who might even have had difficulty in writing at all? One early bishop, Papias of Hierapolis, is responsible for the tradition that Mark wrote down what he heard Peter preach, and from the material he gathered in this way he fashioned the gospel which bears his name, and which does read like an eyewitness account. He used his stumpy fingers to good effect, overcoming any limitations. The example of Mark challenges us to take a positive view of our limitations and disadvantages. Horace Bushnell, a well-known preacher of a former generation, offered a similar kind of challenge. He wrote, 'Never imagine you could do something if only you had a different lot and sphere assigned to you. The very things that you most deprecate as fatal limitations or obstructions are probably what you want most. What you call hindrances, obstacles, discouragements, are probably God's opportunities.'

In our study of John Mark, three factors have stood out: he was a man who profited from his early advantages; he was a man who learned from his mistakes; and he was a man who triumphed over limitations. We are wise, then, not only to read his gospel but to read also the lessons of his life.

SIMON

The zealot

LUKE 6:15; Acts 1:13

Some years ago, a well-known newspaper mounted an exhibition entitled 'Masada'. By means of pictures and archaeological artifacts, it retold the story of heroic resistance put up by patriotic Jews on the rocky fastness of Masada, a natural fortress about three miles from the western shores of the Dead Sea. In AD72 a Jewish force of fewer than a thousand men faced the might of the Tenth Roman legion under Flavius Silva. They held out for a long time within the almost impregnable enclosed area at the top of the rock, but were finally subdued by military machines and the use of fire by the Romans. The victorious Romans, however, were denied the satisfaction of taking living trophies of their triumph. By the time they had broken through the defences, the Jews had died in a mass suicide pact, with the exception of two women and three children who were found hidden in a cave.

Those Jews on Masada belonged to a movement known as the Zealots, a fiercely patriotic group in Israel at the time of Jesus. Different opinions were held about the Zealots. Josephus the historian, for example, vilified the Zealots as ruthless terrorists who acted with irresponsible disregard for the consequences of their actions and, according to him, were in no way representative of Jewish people of their day. Many modern Jews would reject the view expressed by Josephus, and Masada has become a potent symbol of the courage and resilience of the Jewish people in establishing the nation of Israel in this century. F. F. Bruce was convinced that not only was Josephus' picture of the Zealots prejudiced, but it failed to reflect their genuine love of their national heritage in all its forms. They were men of vision who dreamed of a liberated, reformed and religiously-renewed society. They were also well-known for their concern for the poor and worked for the removal of injustice and oppression. This brought them into conflict with the Jewish establishment whose pragmatic collaboration with the Romans helped to facilitate the system which oppressed the poor.

In spite of their high ideals, however, the Zealots were violent and intolerant men who believed in violence as a way of achieving their goals. Some of them were called Sicarii, a name derived from the word for a kind of dagger, a weapon which they carried under the tunic and, if the opportunity presented itself or could be engineered, they would use the dagger to dispatch any Roman soldier or official.

One of the men Jesus called to be a disciple and apostle was a Zealot. In the list of disciples he is called Simon Zelotes. It is possible, therefore, had Simon not become a disciple of Jesus, and had lived long enough, he might have been on Masada in AD72.

In becoming a follower of Jesus, Simon would soon learn that certain features of his Zealot background were incompatible with the teaching of Jesus. There can be little doubt that Simon would need to change. Before he fell under the influence of Christ, Simon would share the Zealot hatred of the Romans, a hatred that could be fierce and all-consuming. But what effect would that hatred have upon his own mind and heart? As a Zealot he wanted to right the wrongs of society, to end oppression and usher in a new age of freedom. In meeting Jesus, he met Someone who was also concerned about the poor and exploited, and who spoke about the Kingdom of God. But that Kingdom was about inner personal goodness as well as social justice. Simon would be made to think about the effects in his own life of all the hating. A life motivated by hatred is a life spoiled by bitterness. It has been said, 'Hatred feeds like a cancer on its host. It is a madness of the spirit, which quenches all pity and corrupts all judgement, it distorts the view of others and coarsens the finer feelings in the soul. Hatred is a spiritual disease.' Hatred will adversely affect the hater far more than the hated; the subject much more than its object. In the gospels Jesus must have surprised His hearers by implying that hatred is a kind of mental murder. When we really hate another person, are we not wishing that person out of existence?

A television news item in September 1988 carried the story of a man whose son had been killed by a drunken driver. It was a particularly callous killing, with the young victim being carried on the bonnet of the car for some distance before falling off, and the driver speeding away from the scene. The dead boy's father, however, did not forget. He bought a van and transformed it into a sophisticated surveillance unit, equipped, among other things, with a telescopic camera and a video camera. Over a period of time he tracked the ex-prisoner who had killed his son and took many incriminating photographs and videos of the man breaking his parole commitment by drinking and driving. With the help of the evidence provided by the man the police were able to secure a further nine months' prison sentence for the offender.

Justice was done and the drunken driver deservedly punished. And yet, as you followed the story, you began to feel that the father had also become a prisoner, a prisoner of his own hatred. The fact that he spent a great deal of money on equipment to ensure that his son's killer would never be able to rest again suggests that his hatred had become a paranoic obsession and he was in bondage to his desire for revenge.

Simon Zelotes came to discipleship with a mind-set that was steeped in hatred. In following Jesus Christ, he would learn a new way and would be set free from the bitterness which was so much a part of the Zealot outlook. He would learn to look at the Romans with new eyes. This did not mean that he would be required to condone the Roman occupation of his country, or to abandon the hope of freedom or become totally depoliticized. It would mean, however, that he would need to see the Romans in a new light; and not as Gentile 'dogs'. The Jesus who healed the Roman Centurion's servant would teach Simon that loving his own people and country did not mean hating people of other nationalities. And insofar as they were still regarded as enemies, then the teaching of Jesus would even require him to love his enemies.

Is there any evidence to confirm that Simon did experience such a change of heart when he became a follower of Jesus? William Barclay shrewdly identified two factors which point to such a change.

First, the fact that Simon was prepared to rub shoulders with Matthew is very significant. Matthew had been a tax-gatherer and this meant that he had been in cahoots with the Romans, helping to run the tax system. Today we would probably regard Matthew as a pragmatist who was making the most of the circumstances. The Romans were there and there was nothing he could do to alter that reality, so it was a case of making the most of a bad job. Matthew had made a good living out of the tax business for himself and his family; he would probably have regarded himself as a realist. But that is not the way the Zealots would have perceived him. To them he was a traitor, and they reserved their deepest resentment for men like Matthew who would be considered as worse than the Romans themselves. It may not be overstating the case to say that in other circumstances Simon might have marked Matthew down as a candidate for the assassin's dagger. Yet, as disciples of Jesus, Simon and Matthew were thrown together in the close companionship of the twelve and this indicates a change in Simon.

A former Ulster paramilitary fighter was converted, and in testifying to the change in his life spoke about the freedom from hatred his new-found faith had brought to him. He said that hatred was no longer the driving force of his life, and he was able to look at former enemies with new eyes.

Secondly, the fact that Simon remained with the disciples after the crucifixion may be another significant clue that he had ceased to be a Zealot. If Simon had only followed Jesus in the hope that Jesus was Himself a kind of Zealot who would eventually grasp political power and usher in the revolution, then the crucifixion would have brought an end to those hopes and to the discipleship of Simon. That did not happen. Simon was still with the disciples after the death of Jesus, and was presumably involved in the work and witness of the Church at Jerusalem. Legend leads us to believe that he later preached in Egypt, and even in Britain. The change that took place in Simon, let it be said, did not mean that a passionate, intense, and purposeful Zealot had become supine and passive as a disciple of Jesus. He was still involved in conflict; not with daggers or swords but with entirely different kinds of 'weapons', those of love and grace and truth. The fervent commitment which characterised Simon as a Zealot would be 'baptized' into Christ and used in His service. William Barclay concluded that since Simon was still with the disciples after the crucifixion then he had come to see that 'the dagger must abdicate for the cross'.

JOSEPH
A disciple in high places
JOHN 19:38; MATTHEW 27:57

William Barclay has pointed out that there are two Josephs in the gospels: one is the Christmas Joseph and the other is the Good Friday Joseph. They appear at the beginning and at the end of the life of Jesus respectively, the one at His birth, and the other at His death. The Christmas Joseph, a just man and a carpenter, helped Mary, his betrothed wife, to lay a healthy baby in a crude manger crib. The Good Friday Joseph, a distinguished and wealthy member of the Jewish Sanhedrin, laid the body of the Saviour in a new tomb. He owned the tomb and it was conveniently near.

It is the Good Friday Joseph we are thinking about in this study, Joseph of Arimathea. As we learn more about him, we are likely to be surprised on four counts.

A DISCIPLE OF CHRIST IN
THE SUPREME JEWISH COUNCIL

Joseph was already a disciple when we first hear of him, but 'secretly because he feared the Jews' (John 19:38b). He moved in the upper strata of Jewish society and is described as a 'prominent member of the Council' (Mark 15:43, NIV). The word used by Mark in this reference has come to mean 'honoured', 'influential'. We might say that he was on the 'front bench' in Parliament. His importance is further underlined by the ease with which he appears to have gained access to Pilate the Roman Procurator, who readily acceded to Joseph's request for the custody of the body of Jesus. It is clear, then, that Joseph was a very important person and he was a disciple.

We generally picture Jesus as a friend of the poor, the poor who 'heard him gladly'. Yet it must not be thought that Jesus was always focusing His concern narrowly on one section of society to the exclusion of the rest. Jesus was not a revolutionary who despised the ruling class. He saw people as people, whatever their social background, individuals with personal needs and a need of the mercy of God. He drew people from every walk of life and every level of society.

He was aware, of course, of the divisions in society and the wide differences between rich and poor, between the privileged and the dispossessed, yet He spoke to the deep needs of the human heart, needs that go deeper than the social or material differences. The experience of an American minister will illustrate the point. His first pastorate was in a fishing village in Massachusetts. His people were manual workers. They were ordinary, down-to-earth folk. The time came for him to move on to another pastorate and he found himself ministering to a different type of congregation in a rather up-market area of a large city. At first he felt intimidated by the prospect of preaching to the intelligentsia. His account of how things went and the discovery he made is worth noting. 'What did I have to say to such people? I soon discovered that I had not really moved at all, only that the people had different names. Scratch a professor and you find a fisherman. He dresses differently, has more words to defend himself with, but he has the same problems, the same fears. He worried about the same things in the middle of the night.'

THOUGH RICH, HE WAS
SEEKING GOD'S WILL AND PURPOSE

Matthew tells us that Joseph was a rich man of Arimathea (Matt. 27:57). The fact that Joseph had bought a tomb in Jerusalem is an indication of his wealth. Yet it seems clear that money and possessions were not the be-all and end-all of life for this member of the Sanhedrin. This is how Luke describes Joseph: 'Now there was a man named Joseph . . . a good and upright man . . . and he was waiting for the kingdom of God.' (Luke 23:50, 51.) The two Greek words used in this description suggest that he was a gracious, kindly (Greek:

agathos) person and a man of high moral principle (Greek: *dikaios*). Then Luke adds a very significant phrase. He says that Joseph was 'waiting for the kingdom of God' which means that he shared the Jewish hope of a coming new era under Messiah's rule.

Joseph's wealth had not made him into a materialist. He retained a spiritual outlook on life and wanted to see God's purpose fulfilled in his own lifetime. Joseph, for all the honour that went with high office and for all the freedom that wealth bestowed, had not lost his sense of values. Harry Emerson Fosdick once said, 'You cannot buy in any market a clear conscience or genuine affection or inward spiritual power or deathless hope. They move in the unpurchasable realm.' He added that 'everything that money can buy depends for its ultimate worth, for the purpose it serves, and for its final effect on human life, upon the things that money cannot buy'. King Louis IX of France was a devout believer and he expressed his own sense of values when he said: 'I think more of the place where I was baptized than of the Cathedral of Rheims where I was crowned, for the dignity of a child of God which was bestowed on me at baptism is greater than that of a ruler of a kingdom.' Joseph of Arimathea is numbered among those rich and powerful people who do not lose a proper sense of what is truly important in life.

CAUTIOUS JOSEPH COULD ACT WITH RECKLESS COURAGE

John's gospel tells us that Joseph had been a disciple 'but secretly because he feared the Jews'. He was committed to being a disciple but privately and discreetly. His admiration for Jesus would have put him at loggerheads with many in the Sanhedrin, and, as opposition to Jesus intensified, to be a known sympathizer with the man from Galilee could have spelled estrangement from his fellow Sanhedrinists, and maybe even danger for Joseph. These considerations had made Joseph very cautious. But a moment came for Joseph, a vivid sense of personal destiny, when he could conceal his feelings no longer. In their determination to get rid of Jesus the Sanhedrin had acted in a manner totally unworthy of the highest Jewish court. They had bribed a disciple to betray his master. They had tried to find false witnesses to testify against Jesus. The trial was a travesty of justice. They had deliberately concocted the idea that He was a threat to Rome in the attempt to pressurize Pilate into taking action against Jesus. They had cynically incited the crowd to call for His execution when Pilate had declared Him innocent of any indictable offence. Faced with this cynical manipulation of the truth, Joseph throws caution to the wind and refuses to back the majority in their call for the condemnation of Jesus (Luke 23:51).

One commentator suggests that Joseph did not openly vote against the rest; he simply kept away from the meeting of the Council when Jesus was on the agenda. This suggestion is both unwarranted and improbable. Had Joseph simply stayed away from the meeting, no one would have known where he stood on the matter. The fact that his stance was known suggests that he had made his view clearly understood: he was not in favour of the proposed course of action.

In standing out against the other members, Joseph showed the courage of his convictions. He refused to 'toe the party line' if it meant acting contrary to his own conscience. He does not at this stage openly avow allegiance to Jesus Christ, but it took courage to register his disagreement especially in view of the fact that Jesus was considered by many in the Sanhedrin to be public enemy number one.

And so it transpired that the man who was a secret disciple 'for fear of the Jews' displayed a rare courage in the most difficult place of all — the Sanhedrin. It is interesting to note that because Joseph was capable of fear it did not mean that he was incapable of courage. As Richter said, 'Courage consists not in blindly overlooking danger, but in seeing it and conquering it'. Joseph might have been a secret disciple, but he was no coward.

HE DECIDED TO END THE SECRECY
WHEN THE CAUSE OF CHRIST SEEMED LOST

When Jesus hung on the cross most of the disciples melted into the background and were ready to seek safety in hiding. Yet this was the moment when Joseph decided to ask for the body of Jesus, and nothing would more clearly reveal his allegiance to Jesus than to take His body, the body of one who had died an accursed death, and lay it tenderly in his own tomb. It did seem a strange time to identify himself openly with Jesus when all seemed lost. You would expect that Joseph might have breathed a sigh of relief that he had not publicly avowed himself a follower of Jesus, now that things had turned out so badly for Him.

During those heady days in Galilee when scores of people surrounded Jesus and acclaimed Him as a great man of God, it would have been understandable if Joseph at that time would have been tempted to be a disciple. The time to nail his colours to the mast was when the ship was in full sail and purposefully going somewhere, not when the ship had run aground on treacherous rocks. Yet it was in the shadow of the cross that Joseph resolved to do something that would identify him with Jesus in a very profound and open way. The question we are bound to ask is, 'Why then? Why then when all seemed lost?'

One possible answer is that Joseph had been so deeply outraged by the dubious tactics of his colleagues in their determination to be rid of Jesus that he felt compelled to do what he could to redress the wrong. This is possible, but the more likely reason has to do with the cross itself. The bearing of Jesus during His trial and the way He died upon the cross, praying for those who crucified Him, exercised a profound effect upon the mind and heart of Joseph. The cross itself became the turning point for him. The courage and selflessness with which Jesus faced death might have brought a sense of shame to Joseph for the way he had kept his allegiance to Jesus a secret. The cross brought Joseph to the point of openly demonstrating his commitment to Jesus.

By offering his own tomb for Jesus, he was assuming the responsibility of a near relative. According to Roman law, the relatives of a crucified criminal might claim the body for burial, otherwise it was simply left as a public spectacle to decompose slowly and serve as a deterrent to others who might be tempted to commit crime. We can only assume that Jesus' own family would have come forward, but Joseph pre-empted any attempt on the part of family and friends. In any case, the family of Jesus would have had the problem of transporting the body back to Nazareth. Thus the opportunity was there for Joseph to assume the role of a near relative and give Jesus a burial with dignity and honour.

By fulfilling the role of a near relative, Joseph was identifying himself with Jesus in the closest possible way. So that after the burial of Jesus, Joseph would be thought of as belonging to the wider family of Christ's followers; he had finally nailed his colours to the mast, finally gone public with his allegiance to Christ. We may think of Joseph, therefore, as the forerunner or even patron saint of all who finally overcome their hesitation and caution — which made them secret believers — to declare openly their faith in Jesus Christ.

LUKE
A doctor and author
COLOSSIANS 4:14

If readers of the New Testament were asked to ponder carefully which of the twenty-seven books that make up the New Testament they could least afford to lose, the Acts of the Apostles would surely be a leading contender for that honour. It is a measure of the greatness and importance of Luke that he has given the world not only his gospel but the book that records the coming of the Spirit and the consequent expansion of the Church. Our indebtedness to him would be difficult to estimate.

There are good reasons for believing that Luke was originally a citizen of Antioch in Syria. Jerome, writing about AD400, echoing the view of Eusebius who wrote 100 years earlier, states that Luke was 'a medical man from Antioch'. If that is the case, then Luke was probably a product of one of the most flourishing churches, with a mix of Jewish and Gentile Christians, a church that became the centre from which the first commissioned missionaries went out to preach the Gospel.

By profession Luke was a doctor. Paul calls him a physician. He was also a painstaking diarist who could research and chronicle events with a sharp eye, and write with a style that still captivates his readers today.

As we try to build a profile of Luke from the isolated references to him and deduce other facts about him from his writings, we may note in the first place . . .

HIS GIFT FOR FRIENDSHIP

For a number of years Luke was a loyal and supportive friend to Paul. We cannot be sure when that started, but we do know that the friendship became a partnership in the Gospel when Luke joined Paul, Timothy and Silas as they were about to sail for Philippi (Acts 16:10, 11). It would not be fair to Luke, in view of his own distinctive contribution to the Christian faith through his writings, to call him a satellite of Paul: it is true, however, that after he joined Paul at Troas he became a close companion of the apostle and travelled with him almost continuously on land and sea. Three things are true of this friendship:

☐ *He was a caring friend.* How do we know this? Luke's concern for Paul's safety was expressed when he joined with others in trying to dissuade the apostle from going to Jerusalem, after the prophet Agabus had predicted dire consequences for Paul if he insisted on visiting the city (Acts 21:10-12). Luke was clearly anxious that Paul's life might be at risk, and so he urged Paul to stay away from Jerusalem. True friends will be protective of one another.

Yet Luke did not try to insist, and when Paul demonstrated his determination to go in spite of the advice given to him, then Luke accepted Paul's decision. This must also be a part of true friendship: the wise friend does not force his or her views on others; friendship is not coercive. A friend takes an interest in you but not a controlling one.

☐ *He was a reliable friend.* Luke was certainly not the kind of friend the writer of Ecclesiasticus warned about, 'Some friends are loyal when it suits them but desert you in the time of trouble' (Ecclesiasticus 6:8, REB). Luke stood by Paul through all the tough times as well as the good, and there were more tough than good times. They were shipwrecked and sea-soaked together, (Acts 27) and Luke was closely associated with Paul during the apostles' imprisonment in Caesarea (Acts 27:1) and later at Rome (Col. 4:14). If it is true that 'prosperity makes friends; adversity tries them', then Luke's friendship with Paul and his other colleagues was tested in much adversity and proved to be genuine.

☐ *He was a reciprocal friend.* The best kind of friendship will have a two-way, give-and-take pattern to it. The friendship between Paul and Luke was obviously of that type. To be with

Paul as a constant companion was a rare privilege, and Luke would learn much from the most theological of the apostles. But it was not one-sided. Luke had his sphere of knowledge, too, in the medicine of the day; he was a master of the Greek language and, if nothing else, his presence and support would have been of great value to Paul. William Barclay speculated, 'Was Luke a doctor who gave up what might have been a lucrative career, to tend Paul's thorn in the flesh and to preach Christ?' It must also have been encouraging to Paul to know that Luke was keeping a careful record of all that God was doing through them and that this might be of great value in the future.

Here, then, is a model for friendship, a giving and receiving kind of friendship. Paul E. Scherer cautioned: 'Friendship has its benefits. But don't try to cultivate any if that's all you have in mind.'

In our appraisal of this remarkable man, we may note in the second place that:

HE DISCOVERED AND DEPLOYED HIS GIFTS

Luke was a born writer. He had a gift for collecting and collating information, and possessed the skill to write narrative in a way that would engage the interest of his readers. This might well have been Luke's outstanding gift, and it was a gift he dedicated to the service of Christ. He discovered his gift and used it. There was a pressing need for someone to chronicle the early history of the Church. Luke was the man with both the skill and the commitment to attempt the task. He did it and did it well.

Luke's example speaks to us powerfully, challenging us to discover and deploy our gifts in the service of Jesus Christ. It may be that you share with Luke the ability to write lucidly and persuasively, and could put pen to paper in the writing of letters or articles, Gospel tracts, books, and so on. It may be that, like Apollos, you have the gift of eloquent speech that stirs the heart and edifies the mind. It may be that, like

Priscilla and Aquila, you have the gift of warmhearted hospitality and could use your home and, by serving people, serve Christ. It may be that, like Andrew, you are gifted with the ability to speak to individuals about the faith. It may be that, like David, you are gifted with musical skills which can be employed in the worship of the Church.

There are those within the Church who feel they have no special talent to offer. They do not perceive themselves as *gifted* in the way that others are gifted. Yet it is surprising how God can use what we have and what we are. When Jesus called the disciples and promised to make them fishers of men, they might have concluded that as fishermen they could offer little to the spiritual mission of Jesus. What Jesus said to them, in effect, was that He would take their courage, persistence and patience — their fishermen's qualities — and use them as useful resources in winning men and women into His kingdom.

A person's gifts, according to Ibsen, 'are not a property, they are a duty'. That is a fine thought, but Christians go beyond that and describe their gifts and talents as a trust from God, a stewardship. We do well to take a leaf out of Luke's book and not allow our gifts to be part of the frozen assets of the Church.

In this profile of Luke, we may note in the third place:

HOW LUKE IS MIRRORED IN HIS WRITINGS

Although Luke set himself to produce an objective and accurate account of the events he records so as to convey 'authentic knowledge' to Theophilus (see the Prologue to his gospel), nevertheless, the material he selects for inclusion in the gospel and in the Acts of the Apostles reflects Luke's own subjective view of Jesus and the Messianic mission. His writings, therefore, tell us first and foremost about Jesus but also something about Luke himself. What, then, can we learn about Luke from his writings?

☐ *Luke had a gospel that embraced the world.* When Luke saw how Jesus reached out to Samaritans, sinners, outcasts, the poor and dispossessed, as well as to people of culture and standing in society, he caught the vision and so was eager to portray Christ as the Saviour or Liberator of all people. Luke wanted to leave the world in no doubt about the universal significance of Jesus Christ.

Rabbi Hugo Gryn has told how his Jewish tradition cherishes the legend which pictures God surrounded by ministering angels who sang and danced after the Children of Israel crossed the Red Sea so miraculously. Then they noticed that God was crying. 'Are you not glad?' they asked. 'How can I rejoice,' asked God, 'when my children are also drowning?' Luke believed that Jesus had come into the world to preach a Gospel that would reach people of every race and nation and class.

Michael Wilcox says of Luke, 'Had there been coffee tables in the homes of the Roman Empire they, I think, would have been one destination which Luke would have wanted his books to reach.'

Jesus' words spoken about Zacchaeus sum it up. Here was a man who was boycotted by respectable Jews, yet Jesus says of him, ' . . . this man, too, is a son of Abraham. For the Son of Man came to seek and to save what was lost.' (Luke 19:9, 10.)

☐ *He stresses the importance of prayer.* The life of Jesus as portrayed by Luke is punctuated with prayer. Jesus prays at His baptism, before choosing disciples, at the Transfiguration, in Gethsemane, and finally on the cross. Without Luke's gospel we should not have had the two parables about the unjust judge and the friend at midnight, both stories emphasizing the efficacy of prayer and the need for perseverance in prayer. Luke was obviously convinced that prayer was a priority in the life and teachings of Jesus.

It is safe to assume, therefore, that prayer was important in Luke's own life and that his work for God, whether as a helper-companion to Paul or as a writer, was all undertaken with prayer. Nor could they have found it easy, always to find time and seclusion for regular prayer given the amount of travelling Luke and Paul did. It would have required a good deal of personal discipline to make time for prayer as they moved from place to place. Maybe Luke realized that the busyness of their lives made all the more necessary the prayer that alone would refuel their fervour.

Luke has learned from the life of Jesus and probably from his own experience, that action and prayer belong together and are not alternative ways of serving God. Action without prayer can soon become human-centred and self-serving; prayer without action becomes detached and ethereal. As Stephen Winward once expressed it: 'Divorced from action, prayer is like a motorist revving up his engine, but never getting into gear and going anywhere.' The need for prayer-inspired action is expressed in an old saying, 'Pray as if everything depended upon God; work as if everything depended on you.' Luke highlights prayer both in the gospel and in the Acts of the Apostles.

□ *He does not marginalize women.* In Luke's birth narrative, Mary occupies a central place in the story. It is to Mary that the angel Gabriel appears. Luke records the words of the prophetess Anna, who 'talked about the child to all who were looking for the liberation of Jerusalem' (Luke 2:38, REB). This must surely mean that she spoke about Jesus in Messianic terms. Luke records her joy in welcoming Jesus matching the joy of the devout old Simeon.

Later in the gospel we read about the visit Jesus made to the home of Mary and Martha. We remember how Martha complained because Mary was not doing a fair share of the work in catering for their guests. But Jesus defended Mary and commended her for 'desiring the better part'. In Mary, Jesus found someone whose heart and mind were responsive to what He was saying about the things of the Kingdom. From the remarks of Jesus we are to conclude that He certainly did not teach that a woman's place is confined to the kitchen. Jesus' attitude to women was very different from that shown by many of the rabbis of His day. One rabbinic authority said that a rabbi would be well-advised not to 'speak much with women'. Those rabbis who took that view would have applauded Martha for insisting that Mary's place was serving tables. Luke grasps the new insights implied in Jesus' response to Martha. Jesus deals with people, whether male or female, as people of equal standing before God and equally able to receive and respond to His teaching.

In our appraisal of Luke, we note finally:

HIS EFFORT TO COMMUNICATE THE FAITH TO ONE INDIVIDUAL

Both the gospel and the Acts of the Apostles were written to one individual, a man called Theophilus. It is perfectly reasonable to assume that Luke was also 'writing for the record' as some scholars believe and that his work would become a reliable account for posterity. Nevertheless, his immediate purpose was to write the life of Christ and tell the story of the early Church for one man.

This Theophilus was probably a man of some standing in Roman society, high-ranking with power and wealth. It is not clear whether he was a committed Christian with incomplete knowledge of the faith or a sincere enquirer. What is not in doubt is that Luke was prepared to take immense pains to enlighten one person.

It might seem an extravagant expenditure of time and effort to write a gospel and a history for the sake of one person. Where had Luke learned such a concern for the individual? Was it not from the One who told the story about the shepherd who went in search of one lost sheep; from the One who chose a form of ministry that would constantly bring Him into contact with individuals? F. G. Peabody said of Jesus, 'He was not primarily the deviser of a social system, but the quickener of individual lives.' There is a story told about Professor Duncan, a great Hebrew scholar of a previous generation. He was good at languages. When he was at Edinburgh he learned that a certain man from the East had been taken into Edinburgh Infirmary suffering from a terminal illness. When he heard about the case, Professor Duncan said, 'I will learn his language that I may tell him about Jesus.' To reach one person, 'Rabbi' Duncan as he was called, thought it worthwhile to go to all the trouble of learning a language. H. Clay Trumball said, 'The world is never going to be brought to Christ wholesale, but one by one.' And there is a bit of financial philosophy which says, 'Take care of the pence and the pounds will take care of themselves', and this may also be true as a philosophy of evangelism: the numerical growth of the Church may be best secured when Christians have a genuine care and love for individuals, and when that happens the numbers will follow!

So we come to the end of this look at Luke. Although the biographical date about him is sparse, we are able to deduce from his writings and from Paul's references to him that he was deeply committed to Christ; that he had a firm grasp of the universal appeal of the Saviour; that he was a spiritual man who understood the importance of prayer; that he worked in tandem with Paul as a close and trusted friend; and that he employed his considerable skills to write a gospel and a history of the early days of the Church initially for the sake of one person. To reflect upon the example of Luke is to be inspired and challenged.

PAUL

A new man in Christ
2 CORINTHIANS 5:17

Tradition depicts him as a small man, yet in influence and achievement he towered over the early decades of the Christian Church. 'In truth,' wrote Dean Farrar, 'it is hardly possible to exaggerate the extent, the permanence, the vast importance of those services rendered to Christianity by Paul of Tarsus.'

To do anything like justice to the apostle Paul, we would need to explore the significance of his early life in the cosmopolitan city of Tarsus; we would need to evaluate his missionary exploits and achievements; we would need to take account of the impact of his letters on all subsequent Christian belief and practice; and we would need to say something about his remarkable faith and the qualities of courage and perseverance that so strongly marked his character. However, the limitations of space imposed by the purpose of this book will not allow such a wide-ranging survey of his life; so instead of attempting the impossible we will focus on one particular aspect, namely, the radical change that took place in Paul when he became a Christian. He was a 'new creature in Christ'. What did that mean in his own experience? At least four things!

HE CHANGED HIS MIND ABOUT JESUS

Before his conversion Paul had learned to hate the name Jesus. As far as he was concerned Jesus and His followers posed a threat to Judaism and he felt fully justified in committing himself to a one-made crusade to wipe out the loathsome sect, not only from Judea, but from Diasporan Judaism as well.

Then came the momentous meeting with the Risen Christ on the road to Damascus, and through that experience he underwent a radical rethink about Jesus Christ. We do not know whether or not this change of mind had been germinating in Paul over a period of time. He had seen Stephen die bravely with an unyielding loyalty to Christ, and he did refer to this when he later recounted the facts of his conversion. This suggests that Stephen's death did impact upon Paul's thinking. What we do know for certain is that on the Damascus Road, and during the days following, Paul abandoned his view of Jesus as the instigator of a subversive movement and came to believe that Jesus was the Son of God. How do we know this? The evidence is very clear. Not long after his conversion, Paul began preaching, and the theme of his first sermon in the synagogue in Damascus emphasized that Jesus 'is the Son of God' and the promised Messiah (Acts 9:20, 22).

To have heard Paul naming Jesus as 'the Son of God' must have astounded both Jews and Christians alike. Leslie Weatherhead believed that one of the strongest evidences for Christ's divinity is the fact that it 'found a home in the minds of Jews who, unlike the Romans and Greeks, with their worship of many "gods", were strict monotheists and all their training and pre-conditioning made them hostile to the thought of a man's divinity'. Paul as an ardent Pharisee would have been a strong monotheist, yet soon after his conversion he is saying about Jesus: 'This is the Son of God' (Acts 9:20, NEB). This was a truly remarkable concept for a monotheist.

In our day there will not be many people who feel as antagonistic towards Jesus as Paul did in his pre-conversion days, yet changing one's mind about Jesus is still an important factor in Christian conversion. When C. S. Lewis, the Oxford scholar and author, became a believer he saw that becoming a Christian involved the acceptance of what the New Testament taught about Jesus Christ. He came to see that Jesus was who, and what, He claimed to be or He was a self-deceived megalomaniac. Lewis realized that he could not simply doff his hat to Jesus as a good man; Jesus was the Son of God, the Messiah and Jewish prophetic expectation, or He need not be taken seriously at all and His claims discounted as preposterous.

Why is it so important for a Christian convert to accept the divine Sonship of Jesus. Dr John Stott answers that question in his book *The Cross of Christ*. He points out that if God had sent a man or an angel we might be grateful but a man or an angel would be a third party. By giving His only Son, God was giving Himself. 'God was in Christ reconciling the world to himself' (2 Cor. 5:19, REB). H. C. G. Moule said, 'A Saviour not quite God is a bridge broken at the farther end.'

HE CHANGED HIS MIND ABOUT SALVATION

There was a time when Paul believed that the way to win the favour of God and secure salvation was all a matter of acquiring personal merit by keeping the law. The law not only told you what you should not do, its *proscriptions*, but also told you what you should do, its *prescriptions*. It laid down how a person should behave within the family, towards neighbours and even strangers. It also gave directions as to how God was to be worshipped. A zealous Jew would strive to adhere both to the original law of Moses and the rabbinical rules which purported to apply the original law to the specific situations of everyday life.

Paul was one of those Jews who were so punctilious in their observance of the law that they were convinced that so far as that kind of legalistic goodness was concerned they could not be faulted (Phil. 3:6).

How could a man like that ever be made aware of his need of the forgiveness of God? Not easily! It would take a revolution in his thinking. For Paul to admit that he was a sinner would be like a High Court judge admitting to criminal conduct. We get a good idea of what Paul was like from one of the parables of Jesus. Two men went up to the temple to pray. One was a tax collector who came to confess himself a sinner in need of mercy. The other was a Pharisee who simply presented to God a glowing report of his own moral and spiritual state. And such a man was Paul before his conversion: he prayed, he fasted, he tithed and kept the law, moral and ceremonial, as perfectly as a human being could.

One of the profound consequences of the Damascus road experience was that Paul gave up his dependence upon his ability to keep the law as the means of gaining acceptance with God. And when he later wrote that Christians are not saved by works or by keeping the law he was not simply doing theology; he was speaking out of the depths of his own experience. In the light that shone around him on the Damascus road, he saw himself as a sinner in need of mercy. This was a decisive change in Paul's thinking, and it was a new way of thinking that would underlie his theology. He would no longer boast about his own goodness; instead he would glory in the cross of Christ and the redemption won for humanity through the sacrifice of the Son of God.

HE HAD A CHANGE OF MOTIVE AND METHOD

In the new life on which Paul had embarked after his Damascus road experience, love became the dominant motive of his life. Where he had been formerly preoccupied with the law, love now became the new principle of life. How are we to account for this change? Paul's letters provide clues. To the new Paul God had become 'the God of love' (2 Cor. 13:11). And this God of love poured out His love into the hearts of believers by the Holy Spirit (Rom. 5:5). Paul speaks of the death of Christ in the most personal terms . . . 'the Son of God, who loved me and gave himself for me' (Gal. 2:20). In his ministry it was the love of Christ which impelled him (2 Cor. 5:14). He insists that love is more important than either knowledge or power (1 Cor. 13:1-3).

Again we need to remind ourselves that this emphasis on love was not merely a grand theological concept or ideal for Paul but a new principle of life by which he lived. This love found expression in the care and concern he showed for many people of widely differing backgrounds and races. Although he became a kind of international Christian and his mission spanned many countries, he never lost the strong personal links with many friends in different parts of the world. He must have had a long prayer list as we learn from his epistles. His Christian love was a love that prayed for others, taught others, forgave others, encouraged others, sometimes admonished others, and always nurtured spiritual growth in others.

Another expression of the principle of love in the new life which Paul had embraced is seen in the contrast between his use of violence in his pre-Christian days when he had attempted to stamp out the Christian movement by putting a number of Christians to death, and the way he renounced violence as having no part in the functioning of a Christian missionary, not even in self-defence. In fact, the apostle Paul urges the Christians at Rome not to seek revenge (Rom. 12:19). It is to Paul that we owe that immortal definition of love. 'Love is patient and kind. Love envies no one, is never boastful, never conceited, never rude; love is never selfish, never quick to take offence. Love keeps no score of wrongs, takes no pleasure in the sins of others, but delights in the truth. There is nothing love cannot face; there is no limit to its faith, its hope, its endurance.' (1 Cor. 13:4-7, REB.)

HE HAD A CHANGE OF MIND ABOUT NON-JEWS

Before his conversion Paul had been a Pharisee and as such was locked into the view that Jews were the chosen people of God, and that the rest of the human race were lesser breeds without the law. In one morning prayer the devout male Jew thanked God he had not been born a Gentile, a woman or an animal. Paul had probably prayed that prayer himself. The belief that the Jew possessed a unique status was deeply rooted in the psyche of Paul. He speaks of a 'barrier of enmity' between Jews and Gentiles (Eph. 2:14, REB). Before Christ came Gentiles were 'excluded from the community of Israel' and were 'strangers to God's covenants and the promise that goes with them.' They inhabited a 'world without hope and without God' (Eph. 2:12, REB). This had been Paul's view of Gentiles. His conversion brought about a radical change in his thinking.

☐ As a 'man in Christ', Paul came to the conviction that God loved men and women of every race. Writing to Gentile Christians in Ephesus and identifying himself totally with them, he speaks of God's 'great love for us' (Eph. 2:4), and the context makes it clear the both Jews and Gentiles were included. In Paul's thinking, Jesus was not simply the Jewish Messiah but the universal Saviour and the cosmic Christ (Col. 1:15-20).

☐ The churches that came into existence as a result of Paul's missionary work were multi-racial in character. New converts shared the same status and privileges within the family of believers, irrespective of ethnic backgrounds. He wrote to the Galatians, 'There is no such thing as Jew and Greek, slave and freeman, male and female; for you are all one person in Christ Jesus.' (Gal. 3:28, REB).

On one occasion Paul was prepared to criticize Peter for allowing himself to be pressurized into maintaining the distinction between Jewish and Gentile Christians by not eating with Gentile Christians. Paul said that this conduct 'did not square with the truth of the Gospel' (Gal. 2:14, REB). Paul himself appears to have been completely liberated in this respect and spent most of his apostolic ministry travelling the world making disciples of Jews and Gentiles. According to Paul the Gospel is 'the saving power of God for everyone who has faith — the Jew first, but the Greek also.' (Rom. 1:16, REB.)

There is an old story of an artist who was commissioned to paint a picture of Jesus surrounded by a group of children. The night after he had completed the picture to his own satisfaction, he had a dream in which he discovered someone colouring in the white faces of the children, making some brown and some others black. 'Stop!' said the artist. 'You're spoiling my picture.' 'On the contrary,' came the firm reply, 'you have spoiled it. Who told you that I loved only white children?' At that point the artist recognized the identity of the stranger. When Paul became a believer in Christ, it was as if God asked him, 'Who told you that I loved only the Jewish people?'

We have looked at four changes that took place in Paul when he became a 'new creature in Christ'. He changed his mind about Jesus Christ and so it followed that from being a persecutor of Christians he became a proclaimer of Christ. Abandoning his dependence upon the keeping of the law as a means of earning merit and impressing God, he came to rejoice in the grace of God as the only hope of salvation. Love became the master principle of his life, displacing the legalism of his Pharisaism. From a narrow preoccupation with his own people, he was given a vision of a needy world to be won for Christ.

So that when Paul describes a Christian as a 'new creature' or, as we might render it 'a new person', it is as much a testimony of his own experience as it is a theological statement. Paul was himself the paradigmatic new person.

STEPHEN

A man full of faith

ACTS 6:5

Stephen is a New Testament figure about whom it is tempting to say 'If only!' If only his life had not been cut short by a premature death, would he not have played a significant part in the expansion of the Church in the first century? The answer is surely that Stephen would, indeed, have become a great apologist for the faith. For one thing he had the right kind of credentials. He probably had strong Gentile connections. The fact that his name was Greek (*Stephanos* is Greek for 'crown') and that he was charged by the church in Jerusalem to ensure that Hellenistic widows were not overlooked in the financial help given to the less privileged of the church suggests that he was a diasporan Jew, a Jew who had spent at least some of his life in a Gentile setting.

If this quite reasonable guess is correct, then it means that with his practical experience of the Gentile world, coupled with his deep knowledge of all things Jewish, Stephen would have made a first-class missionary to the lands of the Mediterranean, just as Paul, Timothy and Apollos, three other diasporans, were able to minister effectively in Gentile churches. That, however, was not to be. Stephen, for the sake of the Gospel, paid the ultimate sacrifice and became the first Christian martyr. It is puzzling to read of Stephen's death so early in the story of 'The Acts of the Apostles' when he might have become a great leader and apologist for the Christian faith. Why was he not miraculously preserved from his enemies? Why were his enemies allowed to put him to death? When we face questions like these we are wise to admit that there are mysteries and ambiguities we cannot unravel, and probably will never understand in this earthly life. It is difficult to understand why James became the first apostle to be martyred when Herod targeted the leaders of the Christian movement, yet Peter was miraculously delivered from prison and escaped from Herod's clutches (Acts 12:1-11). We struggle to understand why one died and the other was delivered. The apostle Paul reminds us that in this life 'we see only puzzling reflections' and 'our knowledge now is partial' (1 Cor. 13:12, NEB). When we cannot understand the things that overtake us, we are wise to trust in the sovereign wisdom of God and believe 'that in everything God works for good with those who love him' (Rom. 8:28, RSV).

HIS FIRST TASK

Stephen first appears on the scene with six other men who were all chosen to do a practical job in the life of the Church. They were commissioned to organize and supervise the distribution of the pooled resources of the Church. A problem had arisen which necessitated their appointment. The problem was this: the Greek-speaking widows were 'being overlooked in the daily distribution'. This could have led to divisions in the Church. The leaders acted decisively to ensure the unity of the Church.

Stephen, in fulfilling this task with the others appointed with him, would be exercising a reconciling influence in the life of the Church in those critical early days of the Christian movement. By ensuring an equitable distribution they were removing any suspicion that Aramaic-speaking Christians from Judea were being favoured over the Greek-speaking widows who were probably diasporan Jews converted to Christ. The injustice needed to be corrected quickly, otherwise the Church would become a community with first-class and second-class members.

Stephen and his fellow deacons were functioning to create unity in the Church, and their example challenges all Christians to work for the unity of the Church in general and their own church in particular. When we see a situation of conflict developing we should ask, 'Am I helping to resolve the conflict or am I making things worse? Am I part of the problem or part of the solution? Am I pouring oil on troubled waters or am I pouring fuel on the fire?' Every Christian confronted with strife in the church or community should be committed to a damage-limitation exercise. 'Blessed are the peacemakers,' said Jesus. Like Stephen, we are to be involved in maintaining the unity of the Spirit in the bond of peace (Eph. 4:3).

HIS MULTI-ROLE

Although Stephen is appointed to do a practical, administrative kind of job, it is remarkable how he combines theological, spiritual and practical elements in his life. He passes easily from the role of caring for the needy as a practical Christian to that of defending the faith as an informed apologist. He was also 'full of the Spirit'. Here this exemplary Christian displays three components: practical service, an intellectual grasp of the faith and life in the Spirit.

One of the mental blocks preventing such an all-round Christian development may well be what we may call the 'either/or' syndrome, which affects those who believe their forte is either to be 'spiritual' or 'practical' but not both. There may be those who are happy with a needle, paintbrush or trowel in their hand. The practical woman will aspire to be like Dorcas in her good deeds or to be like Lydia in the way she extended hospitality to many. The practical man may relate to Nehemiah who built the walls of Jerusalem or Paul making tents. And yet, if the Christian is only a practical Christian, then his or her life is lop-sided; Christian growth is stunted. The Bible never allows us to think that practical service can stand in lieu of a devotional life of prayer and meditation.

The other side of the coin is that other Christians may be strong on the devotional and Bible-study aspect of discipleship, but lacking on the practical side. There is a story from the ancient world about a man called Thales, one of the outstanding early philosophers. One night while looking up at the stars he fell down a well. A little maidservant said to him,

'You're a fine one. You know all about things above your head, and you don't know what's under your feet.' And if we paraphrase the apostle Paul's famous words to the Corinthians, he said something like this: 'Though I am very spiritually minded, though I keep abreast of theological developments and thought I may be the most prayed-up saint around, though I preach with the tongue of an angel, if I do not have love, the love that cares and extends the helping hand, then I am nothing.'

Stephen's example reminds us that the practical and the spiritual are two sides of the coin of true discipleship, and that it is a mistake, therefore, to think that there are two species of Christians, one spiritual and the other practical. He was a man of faith and full of the Spirit and 'he did great wonders and miracles among the people', yet he was also called to do a practical, administrative task as part of his Christian work.

STEPHEN SLANDERED

Just as Jesus had faced false charges, so Stephen became the victim of trumped-up evidence. Men from one of the synagogues in Jerusalem, a synagogue attended by diasporan Jews, bribed witnesses who were willing to swear that Stephen had despised Moses, the Temple, and the law. They deliberately misinterpreted Stephen's meaning so as to secure a verdict against him. In debate with Stephen, these men from the synagogue rejected the claims Stephen made for Christ, 'so scandalous and revolutionary did they appear'. (F. F. Bruce, *The Book of Acts*, Marshall, Morgan and Scott, 1971, page 134.)

It is instructive to notice that the trouble that engulfed Stephen came upon him as a direct result of his Christian witness; it flowed from doing what he perceived to be the will of God for him. Jesus warned His disciples that in the world they would meet with persecution. This is one of the paradoxes of being a Christian: by following Christ a person may be delivered from some troubles such as guilt and fear, and prophylactically saved from others by following a healthy Christian lifestyle, but there may be another kind of trouble that comes as a consequence of a commitment to the will of God. The truth is that these early Christian witnesses would have had a much easier life had they not become Christians. This was probably well understood and accepted by them. When Paul wrote to Timothy he told the young pastor at Ephesus, 'Take your share of hardship, like a good soldier of Christ Jesus.' (2 Tim. 2:3, NEB.) Christianity was a minority religion in the city of the goddess Diana and life would not be easy for Timothy as a pastor of a persecuted minority.

Where Christians try to live out the Christian life in society, they may well meet with problems. A young Christian woman lost her well-paid, high-ranking position because her conscience would not allow her to look the other way when the firm for which she worked used ethically-dubious methods. Similarly, a man lost his job because he dared to raise his head above the parapet and question the tax fiddle that produced lower taxes for all concerned in the firm. These are relatively minor problems compared with the persecutions of those who have suffered and died because they were doing the will of God as they understood it. When Martin Luther King campaigned for human rights in America, as part of what he perceived to be his duty as a Christian, he did it in a non-violent way, and yet he was rewarded by being brutally murdered. These are extreme examples, and most Christians will not be asked to *die* for their faith as Stephen and Martin Luther King gave their lives, but they will be asked to *live* for their faith and be prepared for any difficulties and persecutions that may be involved.

THE APOLOGIST

In reply to the charges levelled against him, Stephen confirmed to his Jewish hearers his own authentic Jewish pedigree by reviewing the history of Israel. He had a shared heritage with these faithful synagogue attenders, yet the way he interpreted their common history was not calculated to win their approval. It seems that one purpose Stephen had in mind was to argue that while it was true that God had greatly blessed, guided and favoured Israel, the presence of God could not be confined within the land of Israel. After all, God had appeared to Abraham, far away from the promised land, and had spoken to Moses from a burning bush, also far away from the promised land. And then, again, Stephen acknowledged that the temple was a focus and symbol of God's presence, but it was naïve to believe that God was confined to a building.

His hearers were not enamoured by Stephen's line of argument and, when he implied that by putting to death Jesus Christ they were only doing what their fathers had done in persecuting and killing the true prophets of old, 'this touched them to the raw', and from that moment Stephen's fate was sealed.

We might think that Stephen's message to those men from the synagogue bears no relevance for us today. But maybe it does say to us that we, too, must resist that way of thinking that would localize God within a building or limit His work and activity in the world to one day of the week. Admittedly, a Church has an important purpose and the vast majority of Christians would want to sing: 'We love the place, O God, wherein Thine honour dwells; The joy of thine abode all earthly joy excels.' (William Bullock.) And we warm to the sentiments of hymnwriter H. R. Moxley who bids us sing, 'Build us a holy house of truth, wherein the blind shall come to see, where age shall hand the torch to youth, and youth shall tell the world of Thee.'

A church building may hold tender memories of fellowship and blessing for those who have worshipped in it through the years. Many have made the response of repentance and faith and come to new life in Christ within a particular church building, and that sanctuary has been a virtual gateway to eternal life. Yet, when all this is said it needs also to be said that God is not confined to a sacred place. Stephen's point needs to be taken on board by Christians if we are to avoid compartmentalizing our lives into sacred and secular. We need to share the vision of another hymnwriter who has taught us to sing, 'So shall no part of day or night, unblest or common be; but all my life, in every step, be fellowshipped with Thee.'

HIS FRUITFUL DEATH

Although Stephen's death, as we have already stated, must have seemed sadly premature to his fellow-believers, the consequences of his death were far more significant than anyone could have foreseen.

☐ Stephen's death became a turning point in the story of the Church, as it triggered a more vigorous persecution of Christians. Following the crucifixion of Jesus and the resurrection-ascension events, Jerusalem had naturally been the place where the disciples met together for fellowship, prayer, and mutual encouragement. The city held many vivid memories for them; the momentous happenings of the past few weeks were indelibly etched on their minds. It was in Jerusalem that Jesus had 'showed himself alive' to His disciples. All the apostles were still in Jerusalem and the wonderful phenomena of the Day of Pentecost, when the Holy Spirit was given, had occurred in Jerusalem, so where else, indeed, would any disciple want to be but in the place where thousands had been converted?

The stoning of Stephen changed all that. His uncompromising speech had provoked a violent reaction that not only led to his own death but, more than ever before, every disciple became *persona non grata* in the city. Jerusalem became a dangerous place for all the followers of Jesus Christ. A considerable number of the believers, though greatly admiring, no doubt, the courage of Stephen, decided that discretion is sometimes 'the better part of valour' and they left the city in search of safer places to live. The stoning of Stephen, therefore, set in motion a large migration of disciples, some of whom reached as far as Syrian Antioch.

Luke tells us that this scattering of disciples served to spread the Gospel wherever they went, and new churches were planted. All this happened as an unforeseen consequence of Stephen's martyrdom. His death may strike us as untimely, yet it was also a fruitful death. God turned the wrath of men to serve His own gracious purposes.

☐ There is a good reason for believing that another probable consequence of Stephen's death was the influence it had upon Saul of Tarsus. Saul was himself a fanatical persecutor of the Church. His controlling passion was to stamp out the last vestige of Christianity. He had 'given his consent' to the stoning of Stephen. It seems, however, that the courage of Stephen and the magnanimity of spirit which he displayed when, with almost his last breath, he prayed that the Lord would forgive his murderers, deeply affected Saul. It is probable that the ferment in Saul's mind that would ultimately lead to his conversion began there as he witnessed the death of Stephen. What is the evidence for this claim? Years later, when Paul told the story of his conversion, he recalled the part he played in Stephen's death (Acts 22:20). The fact that he mentions the stoning of Stephen in the context of telling the story of his own conversion suggests that it had exercised a profound influence upon his own heart. It is interesting to note that Paul refers to the martyrdom itself; that is what remained in his mind. What Stephen had *said* that day would have greatly angered Paul, but what Paul *saw* in Stephen's attitude and bearing haunted him. This suggests that the most effective way of witnessing is for Christians to show the truth of the Gospel in the way they live their lives! The only way to prove the reality and relevance of the Christian faith is for Christians to show by their lives that it produces better men and women.

Stephen is popularly known as the first martyr, and the word martyr is generally understood to mean 'someone who dies for the cause'. The dictionary defines martyr as 'one who undergoes penalty of death for persistence in Christian faith or obedience to the law of the Church or undergoes death for any great cause'. So that when we use the word 'martyr' we picture stonings, burning at the stake, lions in a Roman amphitheatre, or more recent examples of missionaries being killed. In fact, however, the Greek word translated martyr meant a 'witness', and originally had much more to do with living for the faith than dying for it. Stephen was not a martyr because he died, he died because he was a martyr/witness. This can easily be confirmed from the New Testament. When Jesus commissioned the apostles to go into all the world He told them that they would be witnesses for Him (Acts 1:8). They would be 'martyrs' in Jerusalem, Judea, Samaria and the uttermost parts of the world. That is to say, they would witness for, and to, Christ by word and example.

Stephen did not live to see the fruits of his courageous witness. At the time of his demise his words had fallen on deaf ears and his death seemed pointless; a total defeat for Stephen himself and also for the Church. Yet how remarkably fruitful his witness proved to be. His example serves to remind us that when Christians live and speak for God they are not always in a position to know what results will flow from their witness. Stephen's example seems to say, 'Be a faithful witness and God will see to it that your witness will bear fruit.'

CORNELIUS

The centurion

ACTS 10:1-48

There are four centurions mentioned in the New Testament and it is something of a coincidence that all four have something favourable said about them. Three out of the four believed in Christ. Perhaps the most interesting of these is a man called Cornelius, whose conversion is reported in the tenth chapter of the Acts of the Apostles.

From the account given in the Acts, it is clear that Cornelius was attracted to Judaism before he became a disciple of Christ. 'He and all his family were devout and God-fearing; he gave generously to those in need and prayed to God regularly.' (Acts 10:2.) In the time of Jesus the term 'God-fearer' was a technical term used to describe a Gentile who worshipped the God of Israel and who lived, as far as possible, according to the Jewish Torah. God-fearing Gentiles were fringe members of the Jewish community. Was the God-fearing Cornelius a 'God-fearer'? To speak of him as God-fearing does suggest that Luke thought that he was as much a God-fearer as a centurion in the Roman army dared be. If he could be said to be God-fearing then he must have believed in Yahweh. He seems to have embraced the Jewish teaching of the need to help the disadvantaged in society, as he demonstrated by giving generously to those in need. He also accepted the Jewish emphasis upon prayer, since 'he prayed regularly'. Inevitably, this must mean that Cornelius had become disillusioned with the pagan religion of Rome and whatever outward religious ceremonies he would feel obliged to share of the old religion, at heart he had undoubtedly renounced the gods of Rome.

We do not know whether Cornelius had sought a posting to Palestine because he was already interested in the Hebrew faith or, and this is more likely, he had become drawn to

Judaism after arriving in the country. Either way, by the time we are introduced to him in the Acts he had become a devout person with an established habit of prayer.

We look at three factors that stand out in the story of Cornelius:

A MAN WITH THE
COURAGE OF HIS CONVICTIONS

It would take a lot of courage for a Roman centurion to admit an interest in the Jewish faith. Cornelius would be expected to be a model Roman abroad, personifying the spirit of Rome. He was trained and paid to protect and promote the interests of Rome. He would be required to set an example in venerating the Emperor. It is difficult, in fact, to see how Cornelius could be a good Roman centurion and a God-fearer. Some Roman writers were contemptuous of Romans who became caught up with the Jewish religion. E. M. Blaiklock referred to a member of the Flavian family who was accused of 'going astray after the customs of the Jews'. One wonders what the soldiers who were under the command of Cornelius thought of his empathy with the Jewish faith. Did they think him a bit eccentric? Did they think he was betraying Rome? It is very likely, however, that because he was devout he would treat his soldiers with greater sensitivity than he might otherwise have done and this, in turn, would elicit a respect for him. But we cannot know how he could be a God-fearer and a Roman centurion; but he seems to have managed it.

Cornelius is an example of a person who will not be deflected in his search for spiritual reality and the knowledge of God. He was prepared to be thought suspect by his fellow Romans as he ventured on his quest, first into Judaism, and then into Christian discipleship. Fear of how family and friends may react and what people may say, can become a block preventing a person from saying 'Yes' when the call of Christ, 'Come follow Me' is heard. If anyone had reason to think like that, Cornelius had, but he did not allow the 'fear of man' to hinder his search for God.

The second significant thing worth pondering about Cornelius is this:

WEALTH NOT THE SUMMUM BONUM

It seems from the evidence of the New Testament that centurions were well paid and enjoyed a very high standard of living. We may recall from the gospels how rich the centurion must have been whose servant was healed by Jesus. On that occasion, the Jews pleaded with Jesus to help the centurion because, they said, 'he loves our nation and has built our synagogue'. That suggests considerable personal resources. Cornelius himself was very generous in giving to the poor. He also had a number of servants (Acts 10:7). Yet it seems clear from the way he is portrayed in this tenth chapter of Acts that he did not consider money as the great goal of life; it was not the bread of the soul so far as Cornelius was concerned. His spirituality meant that he had other concerns that loomed larger than simply making money. Does he not challenge us at this point?

There is no doubt that money is an important factor in our lives. People who live in extreme poverty are likely to believe, and understandably, that money is the big answer to their problems. The colour supplement of a newspaper carried the story, a few years ago, of men who risked their lives in a disused gold mine in the African country of Niger. It was a deep shaft into which men had to slither to work in galleries whose ceilings were unsupported and liable to collapse at any time. They were there illegally and the risk of death was high. Yet, for every man who died hundreds more queued to take his place in the pit. When asked why he took such risks one man replied, 'I'd rather die at the bottom of the Abdullah Hole than die of hunger in my village.' If that man could have found a handful of gold, he would have regarded it as the panacea for all his problems. Money can, and does, solve many problems. Money can bring to people's lives a degree of dignity and a sense of wellbeing that is often missing in the lives of the very poor. Christians discussing money must face realistically the need for money in people's lives, and not be too ready to equate poverty with virtue.

That being said, however, it is not the whole truth. Money is not the answer to some of the deepest needs of the human heart. Money cannot, *per se*, guarantee happiness; it cannot, *per se*, save marriages; it does not of itself bring life's deepest joys and satisfactions. Cornelius was not seduced by money. By his concern for the spiritual dimension of life, he showed his conviction that there was more to life than money or the things that money can buy. A line of a hymn reminds us that it is possible to be 'rich in things and poor in soul'. Cornelius would be rich in soul, rich in faith, rich in love, and rich towards God. Not only did he keep money in its proper place but used it creatively and generously in helping needy people. Money was his servant and not his master.

The third and final thing that is worth pondering about Cornelius is this:

HE WAS A PIONEER

He was the first Roman convert recorded in the Acts of the Apostles, though not the first Gentile: that honour belongs to the Ethiopian eunuch. There were many sincere people in the ancient world who were disillusioned with the pagan religions of their age. Some of the gods of the Greek and Roman pantheons were depicted as being more capricious and less ethical than the human beings who worshipped them. Thoughtful people such as Cornelius were left with a wistful longing for something better to meet their spiritual hunger and answer their need for a knowledge of the true God, Maker of heaven and earth. There are like-minded people in our day with a wistful longing for something more than materialism and pleasure. The interest in astrology, the occult, Eastern mysticism, and sub-Christian cults may well be an expression of the feeling that there ought to be more to life. Cornelius found the answer in Christ.

We have already noted that Cornelius was a Gentile adherent of the Jewish faith. This was a good preparation for his conversion to Christ. For example, his knowledge of the Jewish law would help him appreciate the message of God's grace. The apostle Paul says that the Law is like a schoolmaster that leads us to Christ. What did he mean? His idea was that the Law makes people aware of the differences between right and wrong and shows them that they are sinners before God. The Gospel of forgiveness makes more sense to those who are aware of their need of forgiveness.

For Peter and the Jewish Christians accompanying him, the conversion of Cornelius and other Gentiles at Caesarea was a turning point, as they realized that Gentiles were to be fully accepted as fellow believers. When it became clear to Peter that they had been filled with the Holy Spirit, he immediately arranged for them to be baptized in water. It was then firmly established in his mind that Gentile believers shared the same status as their Jewish brothers and sisters in Christ. There were to be no Jewish first class and Gentile second class Christians!

It is interesting to compare Cornelius's status as an adherent of the Jewish faith and his new status as a Christian. Even if he had become a full proselyte to Judaism he would still not have been considered a full Jew. He could marry a Jewess but not from the priestly families, a prohibition intended to prevent introducing Gentile blood into the priesthood. Further, a male proselyte, who was not the son of a Jewess, was not permitted to be a member of the Sanhedrin, or to hold any other public office. So that while adherents might be very welcome at the synagogue their position remained somewhat ambiguous. We see how radically different is the case with Cornelius's entry into the ranks of the Christian disciples. He receives baptism, and his conversion is sealed by the Holy Spirit, and so he becomes a brother in the family of Christ where the Jew-Gentile distinction is not significant.

As a convert to the Christian faith, Cornelius would have to work out how he could maintain his loyalty to Rome as a citizen and soldier, and how, at the same time, he could be faithful to his new-found faith in Christ. For him the words of Jesus would have special relevance as he tried to 'render to Caesar what belonged to Caesar and to God what belonged to God'. It was not going to be easy for Cornelius. Many Christians are called to live the Christian life and make a Christian witness in tough circumstances. The challenge has been put like this: 'Bloom where you are planted.'

From this look at Cornelius we have noted three things: he was a man with the courage of his convictions, a man of spiritual values and the first Roman Christian.

TIMOTHY

A youthful pastor

PHILIPPIANS 2:19-22

The finest university, it has been said, is life itself, and the teachers in the university of life are the experiences through which we pass. We learn from others in two ways: the bad examples stand as warnings so that we try to avoid their mistakes; the good examples inspire us to live good and useful lives. Preaching that is based on the characters of the Bible is often of this kind: warning us or inspiring us. For instance, King Saul is a warning to us of the way a person can start out full of promise and potential, yet through disobedience and obsessive jealousy spoil his life and bring misery to his family.

Among those whose lives shine out as fine examples is Timothy. F. F. Bruce said of him, 'Of all the great apostle's associates none seems to have been so dear to him as Timothy.' He was certainly a close friend of Paul, and as we piece together what we are told about him in the New Testament we shall see whether his example is one to inspire us.

TIMOTHY'S ADVANTAGES

☐ There was the advantage of his mixed parentage. His father was a Greek and his mother a Jewess. We do not know his father's name or anything else about him. His mother was called Eunice and his maternal grandmother was called Lois (2 Tim. 1:5). This mixed parentage meant that Timothy could relate easily to either Jews or Gentiles, and that probably meant that he could help bridge the gap between Jewish and Gentile Christians within the Church. To be able psychologically to identify with both Jews and Gentiles must have been a considerable asset to Timothy in his work as pastor and evangelist.

The Church always needs the services of men and women

who can exercise a uniting and cohesive influence within the Church, who stand as link-persons, reconciling those elements which might otherwise prove disparate. In the work of evangelism, it is an advantage if the speaker has some common ground with his listeners and is able to establish a rapport with them. Missionary outreach is usually done best by well-trained nationals who are steeped in the culture, tradition and language of their own people, rather than by foreign missionaries. The missionaries' task is often to train the nationals. Timothy's mixed parentage would have given him an advantage in the way he could relate to the Jews and Gentiles among the people to whom he ministered.

☐ There was the advantage of his early training. Timothy was well versed in the Hebrew Scriptures. His father had either died in Timothy's infancy or, still living, was content to leave the education of the boy to his mother and grandmother. From them he received a thorough grounding in the Scriptures. The apostle Paul reminded him of it in the second letter he wrote to Timothy: 'From infancy you have known the holy Scriptures, which are able to make you wise for salvation through faith in Christ Jesus.' (2 Tim. 3:15.)

Paul obviously considered this early training to be of immense benefit to Timothy. Who can estimate the effects of good early training? It is said that when a child is born among certain Arabs, in the first hour of life the nurse whispers the first chapter of the Koran in the baby's ear. This may be a bit optimistic, but it serves to remind us that from the earliest years a child is susceptible to influence. Sir Alec Douglas Home, former Prime Minister and respected as a statesman for his integrity, acknowledged in a television interview that he owed a great deal to his early training, and especially the influence of his mother, in teaching him the Scriptures and the catechisms. The foundations of his own faith and the values which were later to guide him were laid in those early years.

The influence of parents, however, provides no guarantee

that the child will follow in the way of Christ unless the child responds to that influence. Eunice had a strong faith but she could not believe for Timothy. The young man needed to imbibe what he had been taught and embrace the Gospel for himself; he needed to have a faith that was his own assured possession and not something that was borrowed from his mother and grandmother. God has no grandchildren only children. The Gospel tells us that as many as receive Christ are given the right to become the children of God. In Timothy's case it might have been Paul who had been instrumental in helping him to commit himself in personal faith to Jesus Christ. This conjecture is borne out by the fact that Paul calls Timothy 'my son'. We can trace these two influences behind Timothy's faith: his mother had played her part in teaching him the Scriptures but it also needed the apostle Paul to lead him to a definite commitment.

We move on; Paul sheds light on another facet of Timothy's character which may be expressed as:

HIS CARE FOR OTHERS

Writing to the Philippians, the apostle paid this tribute to his younger colleague, 'I have no one else like him, who takes a genuine interest in your welfare. For everyone looks out for his own interests, not those of Jesus Christ.' (Phil. 2:20-21.)

Of all the helpers surrounding Paul, there was no one like Timothy to whom he could so confidently entrust the spiritual care of the Philippians; no one like Timothy who would suppress his own legitimate interests to serve the Philippians. Even in the work of the Kingdom of God, it is possible to be motivated by self-interest; a preaching gift, a fine singing voice, a flair for writing, and so on, can be used to enhance a reputation. Even the great saints of God have experienced the temptation to allow self-interest to take first place in their lives. From Paul's comment, it seems that he had seen the same tendency in a number of his own helpers. 'For everyone looks out for his own interests.' Timothy, however, was showing himself to be the true servant of Christ, reflecting the selfless concern for others which was so characteristic of the ministry of Jesus.

It may be worth pointing out that self-effacing concern for others, as shown by Timothy, does not mean self-obliteration. Timothy would have his own legitimate needs and personal concerns. It is a matter of priorities and balance. The ideal is given in the great command of Jesus. We are to love God first and then our neighbour as ourselves. Note what is said in that command, 'to love our neighbour *as ourselves*'. There is a sense in which we are to love and value ourselves, but that legitimate love of self is subordinated to the purpose of God and the purpose of God prioritizes love for others. Timothy exemplifies the ideal of love for God which expresses itself in a genuine care for others.

Another facet of Timothy's character which is suggested by the words of Paul in our text is this:

HE WAS CONTENT TO PLAY A SUPPORTING ROLE

As a 'son' to Paul, Timothy had learned to be submissive and was prepared to co-operate fully with the apostle. In the first century every child of noble birth was taught obedience to parents as a priority in his or her education. Timothy was happy to work with Paul 'like a son working under his father' (Phil. 2:22, REB). The image Paul uses here is of a family business with the son playing his full part under the general oversight of his father. Timothy was well content to work under the guidance of the apostle. Questions of status and a pecking order do not usually arise in a flourishing family business.

The friendship of Paul and Timothy is a splendid example of how the generation gap can be effectively bridged. Paul valued Timothy and set great store by the work done by the younger man. He did not despise Timothy's youth. For his part, Timothy loved and respected Paul whose learning and experience were invaluable to him.

When a number of architects submitted a design-plan for the Anglican cathedral in Liverpool at the beginning of this century, they were required to do so under *noms de plume* so as to preclude any possibility of favouritism. When a committee of three experts finally agreed on their choice, we can imagine their surprise when the successful architect turned out to be a young man of 21 years of age. Just as a cathedral needed the talent of a young man, so does every church need the gifts of its young people.

Paul appreciated his younger colleague, but it was not one-sided; Timothy knew how much he needed the apostle. Younger people help to remove the generation gap by keeping strong links with the older generation with its wisdom and experience. God has intended that the Church should not be divided in any way. There is always a danger of separation developing between the generations, but it can only result in the impoverishment of all concerned. How enriching for the life of a church or community it is when there is mutual dependence between the age groups. One advantage of such co-operation is that the older are saved from settling down in a rut; the younger are saved from the mistakes that arise from inexperience. One generation needs another. 'For Christ is like a single body with its many limbs and organs, which, many as they are, together make up one body.' (1 Cor. 12:12, NEB.) Any church which shows itself to be a united, all-age family becomes a model of what God intends for His people.

So we come to the end of this brief study of Timothy. It has become clear that he was an important figure with many fine qualities: his genuine desire to serve others, his faithfulness, and his willingness to work under the leadership of Paul set before us not only a character to admire but an inspiring example to follow.

BARNABAS
Son of encouragement
ACTS 4:36

When missionaries first carried the Gospel to the continent of Africa, some Africans marked their conversion to the Christian faith by adopting biblical names. This practice of assuming new names as they embarked on new lives had very good Scriptural precedent. Jesus gave Simon the new name of Peter. In fact, the idea of a 'Christian name' originated with the new name given at baptism. The new name was intended to be a sign of new life in Christ.

The man we know in the New Testament as Barnabas was previously called Joseph, but was given the name Barnabas by the apostles. The name Barnabas literally translated would read 'son of prophecy', but since the main purpose of prophecy was to encourage, Luke freely renders it as 'son of exhortation' or 'son of encouragement'. It is possible that the apostles gave him this name soon after his conversion to the faith, and then the name would always serve as a challenge — a name to live up to. When Martin Luther King received the Nobel Prize he commented: 'I feel as though this prize has been given to me for something that has not yet been achieved. It is a commission to go out and work harder for the things in which we believe.'

He had been given the name of supreme worker for peace and justice; he was determined to live up to the name and prove himself worthy of it. Barnabas was given the name 'son of encouragement'. He lived up to his name in at least three remarkable ways:

HE ENCOURAGED THE NEEDY

In the early days of the Church there took place what has been called 'an experiment in Christian communism'. Luke gives an account of this in the fourth chapter of the Acts of the Apostles: 'for they had never a needy person among them, because all who had property in land or houses sold it, brought the proceeds of the sale, and laid the money at the feet of the apostles; it was then distributed to any who stood in need.' (Acts 4:34, 35, NEB.)

Among those who acted with bold and reckless generosity was Barnabas. He was probably one of the richest men among the first disciples and is said to have 'owned an estate'. He sold it all and donated the proceeds to the pool from which money was then shared with those who were in need. Barnabas stood by the needy, not merely with verbal encouragement but with practical help. James had something to say about this kind of help in his epistle. 'Suppose a brother or a sister is in rags with not enough food for the day, and one of you says, "Good luck to you, keep yourselves warm, and have plenty to eat," but does nothing to supply their bodily needs, what is the good of that? So with faith; if it does not lead to action, it is itself a lifeless thing.' (James 2:15, 16, NEB.) Certainly Barnabas' faith led to compassionate action.

In setting this example of Christian giving, Barnabas touches a sensitive nerve. For most people, self-preservation and self-interest remain the natural priorities of life. It is very natural to regard the resources we have acquired by honest endeavour as our own. It runs counter to our human inclinations to weaken our own position by giving to others. Yet Christian love inspires us to transcend human inclination, to act with a generosity that seems almost irresponsible.

A widow casting her only coin into the offering box was not acting very 'sensibly'. And while it is true that the experiment in pooling resources in early Acts might have been short-lived, the principle of the strong helping the weak — which prompted that experiment — was never abandoned, and was later reaffirmed in the way the churches across the Mediterranean world gave generously for the poor in Jerusalem.

By his willingness to share his wealth with the poor,

Barnabas was living up to his name; he was an encourager of the needy. He challenges us, if not to do exactly what he did, at least to respond as best we can to the needs of the deprived, whether they are near or far away.

Barnabas lived up to his name in a second way:

HE ENCOURAGED THE NEWCOMER

When Saul of Tarsus became a Christian, there were those in the Church who, perhaps not surprisingly, found it difficult to trust the man who had previously persecuted them fiercely and obsessively. How could they be sure that this change of heart was genuine? Was Paul up to something? Was he, just as the occupants of the Trojan horse deceived Troy, trying to infiltrate the ranks of the believers the more effectively to destroy the Christian movement from within? Some of the Christians at Jerusalem were suspicious of him when he visited the city as a new convert.

It was at this point that Barnabas, a highly regarded member of the Church, came forward and interceded on Paul's behalf. He introduced him to the apostles in Jerusalem, convincing them that Paul's conversion was genuine (Acts 9:27). It is doubtful whether Paul would have come to prominence and enjoyed the support of the apostles had not Barnabas opened doors for him. God used Barnabas to prepare the way for Paul. It was by invitation of Barnabas that Paul became associated with the church at Antioch, and it was there in Antioch that Paul received the commission from the Holy Spirit, through the Church which gave him the authority to embark on his missionary work.

As we picture Barnabas welcoming the newcomer and encouraging him to use his gifts in the service of Christ and His Church, are we not challenged to rethink our own attitude to the newcomer? An influx of new people into a church is sometimes seen as a threat to the longstanding members in the circle of fellowship. 'Things will never be the same,' comments an older member. There may be resentment when newcomers are given responsible roles in the life of the church. That was not how Barnabas reacted. He rejoiced that a man with a great intellect and outstanding leadership potential had been converted to the faith. With the world to be won for Christ, why should he do anything other than rejoice? There is room and work for everyone.

Yet Barnabas could have seen things in a different way had he so chosen: he might have been jealous of Paul as a possible rival who could so easily become more popular and more influential among the people at Antioch. With Paul's obvious gifts, he could so easily become the dominant partner, which, in fact, is what did happen. If such thoughts did occur to Barnabas they were ignored by the big-hearted son of encouragement. His all-consuming concern was for the cause of Christ, and this left no room for personal rivalry.

Because the cause meant more to Barnabas than his own status and popularity, he was able freely to encourage Paul to share fully in the work of the Gospel. He probably reasoned that if the intellectual ability Paul had displayed as a Rabbi were redirected into the service of Christ, then to encourage Paul was not only to be magnanimous to a former enemy but was in the best interests of the Church.

Here we touch upon one of the important functions of encouragement: to identify and mobilize the abilities and gifts of committed Christians, gifts which, for one reason or another, have been allowed to remain dormant. In every Christian church there are untapped resources, 'the frozen assets of the Church', which need to be released and used in the multi-faceted work of God's Kingdom. There are natural gifts such as a fine intellect, an ability to communicate, a good singing voice, and so on. There are also spiritual gifts which are given by the Holy Spirit, such as wisdom, healing and inspired insight. Both natural and spiritual gifts are essential within the life of the Church. If Christians are to be more than spectator supporters of the Church, their gifts must be discovered and deployed. We have before us, then, the marvellous example of Barnabas, who recognized in Saul of Tarsus great possibilities and potentialities, and paved the way for the newcomer to use his gifts.

Finally, Barnabas lived out the meaning of his name in one other significant way:

HE ENCOURAGED THE MAN WHO HAD FAILED

The man in question was John Mark who accompanied Paul and Barnabas on their first missionary journey. He stayed with them in their preaching through Cyprus, but when they proposed to go farther afield into Asia Minor his resolve weakened and he decided to return to Jerusalem, and so may be said to have betrayed the faith they had put in him.

Paul was deeply disappointed. The apostle probably reasoned that if they had been guided by the Holy Spirit in taking John Mark with them in the first place, then his leaving them halfway through the project was tantamount to an act of disobedience. Paul felt so strongly about Mark's 'desertion' that when, some time later, Barnabas was in favour of taking Mark on another missionary venture, Paul refused to trust him a second time. Barnabas, however, was equally adamant in his insistence that John Mark should be given another chance, and declared his intention to take Mark with him in spite of Paul's opposition. Neither Paul nor Barnabas was willing to give way on the matter and it caused a rift between them. Barnabas went his way with Mark while Paul went his way with Silas.

It stands to Barnabas' credit that he was prepared to take a risk and put trust in Mark a second time. In the event, his confidence was fully vindicated and he, rather than Paul, was shown to be right. Mark went on to become a most useful servant of Jesus Christ. Indeed, when Paul was later a prisoner at Rome we find that Mark was with him and the apostle was planning to send him on a mission to Colossae (Col. 4:10).

The man who had once failed had become the trusted colleague.

Barnabas knew Mark well (according to Colossians 4:10 they were cousins) and believed in him at a time when he was discredited. The confidence Barnabas placed in him helped to restore Mark's own confidence and served as a spur to renewed commitment. Barnabas understood the truth that God's forgiveness not only wipes out our failures but makes possible a new beginning. It was what Jesus did for Peter after he had denied his Lord; it was what Barnabas did for John Mark.

This, then, was Barnabas. We have seen how remarkably he lived up to the name given to him by the apostles. He was a true 'son of encouragement'. He encouraged the needy by helping to meet their needs. He encouraged the newcomer by finding a place for him in the fellowship and work of the Church. He encouraged the man who had failed by giving him another chance. Barnabas was indeed an encourager *par excellence* and remains an outstanding example to all who make his acquaintance on the pages of Scripture.

SILAS
A man for all seasons
ACTS 15:31, 32

Silas was an honoured member of the church in Jerusalem. His name is taken by the majority of commentators to be a variant of Silvanus. Jerome thought that Silvanus was the Latinized form of Silas and that we are to regard Silas and Silvanus as one and the same person. We know nothing of his conversion, but he soon became one of 'the chief men among the brethren'.

In his time he worked closely with both Peter and Paul. He possessed the gift of prophecy, which he used to good effect to encourage the Christians at Antioch. His importance can be measured by the three jobs he was called to do.

A CHURCH DIPLOMAT

As the faith spread into Gentile territory, the believers in Syrian Antioch were the first to be embroiled in the dispute about the status of Gentile Christians. The first-ever major Church Council was convened at Jerusalem to try to resolve the difficulties, and the outcome of its deliberations was anxiously awaited at Antioch. In brief, what they were waiting to hear from the leaders of the Church was this: Did a Gentile convert need to be circumcised? Had the Council of Jerusalem (Acts 15) insisted on the circumcision of Gentiles, it would mean that at least a male Gentile would have to become a Jew first before becoming a Christian. The issue was hotly debated before a formula was worked out. Gentile converts were asked to respect the law but were not required to be circumcised. This was a momentous decision and it ensured that Christianity would not simply be a sect within Judaism, and that baptism and not circumcision would be the initiatory rite of the Christian faith.

Silas and Judas were appointed to go to Antioch to convey

the decision of the Council and act as spokesmen for the apostles. There was no way of knowing how the church at Antioch would react to what had been agreed, and the situation called for someone with wisdom tactfully to explain what the apostles had written in their letter. Cometh the hour, cometh the man. Silas was the man for the task. The choice of Silas for this kind of role provides a clue to his qualities.

☐ He could be relied upon to expound the directives sent by the Council without adding or taking away from them.

☐ Silas was obviously considered by the apostles to be wise and sensitive. He would exercise a calming and reassuring influence back in Antioch and thus avoid any rift between Jewish Jerusalem and Gentile Antioch. Silas played his part in preserving the unity of the Church at a critical time.

The circumcision controversy was settled, but in the ongoing life of the Church there have never been lacking issues which have caused dissension, and there will always be need for men and women who, as peacemakers, seek to bring a reconciling influence into those tensions.

The second big job fulfilled by Silas was that of

A MISSIONARY

It all came about through an unfortunate set of circumstances. Paul and Barnabas had a disagreement over John Mark, who had 'deserted' them on their first missionary journey. Some time later, Barnabas insisted that Mark should be given another chance and was already planning to take him on his next missionary venture. Paul disagreed with Barnabas and was resolutely opposed to taking Mark with them. He felt so strongly about it that he separated from Barnabas and elected to take as his helper, Silas, who had stayed on at Antioch after giving his report from Jerusalem

This invitation for Silas to join him might have been a strategically-shrewd move on the part of Paul. For Silas to be involved in the missionary outreach from Antioch into the Gentile world meant that one of the 'chief men' from Jerusalem was now associated with the mission. Paul himself was not a Jerusalem figure, and Barnabas was from Cyprus. To have Silas firmly 'on board' would demonstrate conclusively that the missionary enterprise was a matter for the whole Church, including 'headquarters' at Jerusalem, and not just a maverick activity emanating from an upstart Antioch. It was a task given to the Church by Jesus Himself (Acts 1:8), and set in motion by the Holy Spirit (Acts 13:2), and was now clearly supported by the church at Jerusalem. This is not to say that Paul was merely being politically canny. The commitment and missionary zeal of Silas would still be the prior requirement from him. Nevertheless, the Jerusalem 'pedigree' of Silas would give the mission an added authority, and would also serve to remind the church back in Jerusalem that world evangelism was their responsibility, too.

One of the things to emerge from Silas's work as a missionary was the pattern of success and setback with which he had to come to terms. Take, for example, their experience at Philippi. What wonderful encouragement they must have derived from the numbers of converts brought into the faith! How inspired they must have been by the way the church began to take shape as a result of their pioneering work in that city. It was real success by any standards. Yet, there in that same city, they were hounded and thrown into prison. It was there, in chains, and with unshakeable faith, they sang praises at midnight. They did not blame God for their plight; nor did they assume that for this kind of calamity to overtake them they must have strayed out of God's will. They knew that opposition and persecution might come as a result of doing God's will. In fact, they were obviously rejoicing in the confidence that their communion with God was as real in that prison as anywhere else. The apostle Peter wrote, 'But if anyone suffers as a Christian, he should feel no disgrace, but confess that name to the honour of God.' (1 Peter 4:16, NEB.)

Paul and Silas experienced the same pattern of success and setback at Thessalonica. Many converts were brought together to form the church and they appear to have come from all strata of Thessalonian society. This must have thrilled the two apostles, but Jewish opponents deliberately provoked an uproar and Paul and Silas were persuaded by the believers to leave the city under cover of darkness (Acts 17:10). Even for missionaries with indomitable courage, it seems that there are times when discretion is the better part of valour.

Silas proved to be a worthy and durable missionary who was willing to accept the rough with the smooth, success and setback, as part of the inevitable pattern of pioneer missionary work. All who share in the mission of the Church need something of the resilience of a Silas, a resilience which perseveres with the God-given task, without becoming inflated with success or deflated by failure.

The third big job fulfilled by Silas was that of . . .

AMANUENSIS

The apostle Peter ended his first epistle by acknowledging the help he had received from Silas, or Silvanus as he calls him, in writing the letter: 'I write you this brief letter through Silvanus, whom I know to be a trustworthy colleague . . . .' (1 Peter 5:12, REB.)

This Silvanus is widely believed to be the same Silas who accompanied Paul. If this is the case, then it means that Silas was associated with the two major figures of the Apostolic Church, having worked closely with both Peter and Paul.

In what way did Silas help Peter to write his letter? Did he simply write down what Peter dictated? That is possible, but many believe that Silas played a greater part than that of a mere penman. It is more likely that he assisted Peter in composing the letter, and the excellent Greek of the epistle is usually attributed to Silas, who would have had the benefit of a good education as a Roman citizen. In this case, Peter employed the gifts of Silas just as someone today may be employed as a ghost writer.

Silas was willing to use his talents wherever they could

be deployed; whether it was as spokesman for the Jerusalem church or as an assistant missionary to Paul, or as amanuensis for Peter; he was ready to fit in wherever he could be useful in furthering the cause of the Gospel. That Silas was a junior partner to the apostles was something he obviously accepted without resentment. He was content to fill a supporting role. The truth is probably that men like Peter and Paul would not have been as effective without the back-up support of helpers such as Silas. He was content to move in the shadow of the apostles and play his part as a helper. When we are prepared to place whatever gifts we have at the service of Christ, then we shall have something in common with Silas.

APOLLOS
The eloquent preacher
ACTS 18:24

Apollos was a Jew reared in the Egyptian city of Alexandria. The city, which was a banking capital and a focus of considerable trade, was a centre of learning and has been described as the 'University of North Africa'. It had a strong Jewish community whose scholars had produced the Greek version of the Old Testament — the Septuagint. There on the African coast, Greek and Jewish culture met, and there Apollos was brought up.

Of the circumstances surrounding Apollos' conversion to the Christian faith and of the people who influenced him, we have no knowledge. From the lips of some anonymous Christian, Apollos heard the story of the life, death and resurrection of Christ, and from his own knowledge of Messianic prophecies recognized that the person they were describing was the Messiah. Apollos became a Christian.

HE HAD AN INCOMPLETE UNDERSTANDING
OF THE CHRISTIAN FAITH

When he came into contact with Aquila and Priscilla and they heard his exposition of the faith, they spotted the gaps in his knowledge.

□ In some respects, Apollos was well-informed. He was thoroughly acquainted with the Old Testament and this is no more than we would expect given his background as an Alexandrian Jew. The Jewish rabbis in Alexandria had developed the allegorical method of interpretation. That is to say, they took the historical events of the people of Israel and read into them a symbolic meaning. Sometimes their interpretations were contrived, but they always tried to make the Scriptures relevant.

With that kind of background, Apollos was well qualified

to see allusions to Christ in many parts of the Old Testament. This meant he was especially equipped to take up the difficult task of preaching Jesus Christ to the Jews and to convince many of them that the Messianic prophecies had been fulfilled in Christ. This was Apollos' strength. Martin Luther believed that it must have been Apollos, with his broad grasp of the Old Testament, who wrote the epistle we know as Hebrews.

☐ If Apollos was well versed in the Jewish antecedents of the Christian faith there were other aspects of the Gospel in which his knowledge was incomplete. For example, he did not appear to have heard of Christian baptism.

It may be worth pausing to ask whether our understanding of the faith is lacking in certain respects. Apollos was not the first nor would he be the last to have theological 'blind-spots'. For example, if we see the Gospel only in terms of a Good Samaritan concern for the oppressed and underprivileged, we proclaim a purely *social* gospel which omits the spiritual and moral revolution implied in Jesus' teaching about new birth. On the other hand, if we understand the Christian evangel exclusively as the means by which God rescues souls for a redeemed life in heaven, we equally preach a truncated gospel. The purpose of God in the Gospel is both evangelical, in that it stresses salvation for the individual, and social, in that its love-of-neighbour ethic lays the foundation for a just and caring society. The world needs a whole Gospel for the whole person, and that requires the Church to proclaim the '"whole counsel of God"' (Acts 20:17, RAV).

If he was an example of a man who needed to be taught more fully in the faith it is no less true that . . .

HE WAS WILLING TO BE TAUGHT

When he came to Ephesus (Acts 18:24-28) he used his privilege as a Jew to speak in the synagogue. A Christian couple, Aquila and Priscilla, heard his address and invited him to their home to discuss those doctrinal gaps. It's worth noting the discreet and sensitive way Aquila and Priscilla attempted to help Apollos. They did not stand up in the synagogue to expose what was lacking in his teaching for that could have embarrassed him and might have discredited him in the eyes of the other worshippers. Advice and correction, where they are appropriate, are better given privately.

Apollos, for his part, does not seem to have resented being told that he still had much to learn. Maybe he was himself aware of that already and was obviously willing to be taught. What is so remarkable about the attitude of Apollos is that although he probably had a much greater intellect, and was a finer orator than his mentors, he was willing to sit at their feet and learn from them.

No one has a monopoly of knowledge. If we have the humility of Apollos we can learn much from others in our exploration of truth. Apollos reminds us that there is a time to listen as well as a time to talk, a time to receive as well as a time to give.

In the third place we may note:

HE WAS A WISE AND DISCERNING LEADER

This view of Apollos as a wise leader may be illustrated from his relations with the church at Corinth. At one stage Paul urged Apollos to return to Corinth, but Apollos did not think it was appropriate. In fact he was so sure that such a visit would be inopportune that 'he was quite determined not to go' (1 Cor. 16:12, REB). What was it that so convinced Apollos that a return visit to Corinth would be ill-timed? We can only guess. We can confidently dismiss any suggestion that Apollos was too proud to take advice from Paul. We have already seen how graciously he received advice from Aquila and Priscilla.

The most likely explanation of his reluctance to return to Corinth is that he wanted the Corinthians to sort themselves out over the vexed question of factions within the church, which had split the church into three or even four groups.

One party had made Peter its hero; the second group regarded Paul as the chief apostle; while a third party professed allegiance to Apollos himself. Peter's supporters would insist on his primacy, no doubt from the fact that he had been with Jesus, while those who supported Paul would point to the phenomenal achievements of their champion as a missionary to the Gentile world, and those who regarded Apollos as supreme would praise his learning and eloquence.

Apollos was well aware of these cliques and well aware of the dangers of division and idolatry inherent in the kind of personality cult that had emerged at Corinth. For Apollos to have returned to Corinth as Paul had suggested could have revived the party squabbles. It might well be the case, therefore, that Apollos was convinced that the best interests of the church would be more effectively served by his absence than by his presence at that particular time. He decided not to risk disturbing the church and decided to stay away.

If this conjecture is accepted as the most likely explanation of Apollos' decision not to return to Corinth, then the example he sets us is worth pondering. It means that his chief concern was not with his reputation and advancing his own ministerial 'career' but with the wellbeing and the cohesion of the Church, and he places this priority above any desire he might have to return to a church in which he was held in high esteem.

Many of the tensions which arise in church life through jealousy and rivalry would disappear at a stroke if Christians would allow the purposes of God for the church and for their lives to take precedence over personal vanity and the desire for prominence. When Christians can subdue the craving for superiority and admiration, they are better able to work with others for the Kingdom of God.

So we come to the end of our look at Apollos. He was a man whose natural gift of eloquent speech was baptized into Christ and used in the proclamation of the Gospel. He was a man who began to witness to the truth of the Gospel even before he was fully informed in it. He was willing to be taught even by those who might have been intellectually inferior to him. And he was a man who placed the progress and unity of the Church above his own desires. There can be little doubt that Apollos is still teaching us today, and his example is no less eloquent for us than his words were in the first century.

LYDIA
A liberated woman
ACTS 16:14

When Paul visited Philippi, his first audience was a group of women who had come together for prayer on a riverbank outside the town. The apostle did not hesitate to begin his missionary work at Philippi with these women. This illustrates clearly that Paul was not the misogynist he is popularly thought to be. Nor did he share the rabbinic aversion to teaching women. He is obviously pleased to meet the women of Philippi, and is keen to win converts from among them.

One of the women who responded wholeheartedly to Paul's message was Lydia, and Lydia is interesting for several reasons.

A PROSPEROUS WOMAN
WHO HAD SPIRITUAL ASPIRATIONS

Her story begins in what was then called Asia Minor (which was a part of modern-day Turkey), in the town of Thyatira. The town was a centre of manufacturing dyed garments. Lydia was seemingly involved at the selling end of this trade, and in developing her market had moved to Philippi. She was either serving as a sales representative for a Thyatiran firm or she had her own business selling purple made in Thyatira. Either way, she was obviously quite prosperous and appears to have lived in a spacious house in Philippi.

Although she was a successful businesswoman, Lydia was not materialistic in the sense of living only for material things, with a blinkered preoccupation with making profit. We know that she was a seeker after God and that she had probably turned away from the pagan religions of the Gentile world to find a spiritual home in Judaism, worshipping the One God, the God of Abraham, Isaac and Jacob. She was a 'God-fearer', a technical term for a Gentile who became an adherent of the Jewish faith.

However busy and demanding her work might be, she set aside time and space for prayer. Maybe she had learned by experience that in prayer her soul was 'restored' amid all the pressures of her business life, and with the help of prayer she might have found that she was better able to preserve a right sense of values. So it was, then, that when Paul met Lydia she was at prayer with other women beside the river outside Philippi.

Lydia did not expect that money could meet her every need. A modern writer has pointed out that money can buy everything except love, freedom and immortality. Lydia kept alive a deep interest in the things of the spirit and resisted the temptation to become a slave to her business interests. She demonstrated by example how a person can be committed and diligent in business without allowing it to monopolize the whole of life.

She is of interest to us in the second place because:

THE 'HALF-JEW' BECAME FULLY CHRISTIAN

We have already seen that when Paul met the group of women at prayer it was near the riverbank outside the city gates. Their meeting in the open air probably indicates that there was no synagogue at Philippi, and this, in turn, suggests that there were fewer than ten male Jews permanently resident in the city, the quorum required by Jewish law for the formation of a synagogue. So we find a number of women, Jewesses and God-fearers, engaging in some form of worship and prayer.

But why, it may be asked, did that company of women not meet in Lydia's house? The Christian group did so. Indeed, it might be said that the Philippian church was born in her house. Why, then, did the Jewish women not meet in Lydia's house? One possible explanation is that while her Jewish friends welcomed Lydia as a God-fearer, they stopped short of actually using a Gentile's house for prayer. If this is a correct guess, then it means that there was a reluctance to regard her as a full member of the Jewish faith and community; in their eyes she still lacked a genuine Jewish pedigree. The difference remained.

We may note a contrast at this point: in spite of a clear commitment to the Jewish faith, she was still on the fringe, so to speak, whereas when she believed in Christ and was baptized she became as much a Christian as Paul or Silas, enjoying the full status of a Christian. She had become a sister in the family of Christ, a member of the Church of Christ and an heir to all the promises of God. The apostle and his colleagues had no inhibitions about using her home, so graciously made available, as the venue for the first meetings of the embryonic church in Philippi.

It is one of the glories of the Church of Jesus Christ that those who embrace the Gospel become brothers and sisters within the family of God, irrespective of their colour, class or credentials. In the Church today, new converts become part of the Body of Christ with no different status from those whose ancestors have been Christians for generations.

It is important to note the way Luke characterizes Lydia's conversion as something that God has done. He puts it like this: 'The Lord opened her heart to respond to what Paul said. She was baptized, and her household with her.' (Acts 16:14, 15, REB.) This reminds us that bringing men and women to a decision for Christ is not a purely human activity. When the Gospel is preached from the pulpit or passed on person-to-person, the messenger is always dependent upon the Holy Spirit to 'open' the hearts of the hearers.

Lydia is of interest to us finally because:

SHE EXPRESSED GRATITUDE IN A PRACTICAL WAY

After her baptism, Lydia expressed her gratitude for the new life on which she had embarked by inviting Paul and his companions to her home, not only for a celebratory meal but to be her guests. They had already been in Philippi for several days and might have suffered from inferior board and lodge — an occupational hazard for a pioneer missionary. We can almost hear Lydia saying, 'No more of that! You must stay with us.' Lydia implored them to stay at her home. She made them feel that their presence in her home would be a great honour to her and her family. She said, 'If you have judged me to be a believer in the Lord, I beg you to come and stay in my house.' (Acts 16:15, NEB.) There follows an interesting comment by Luke. He says that she pressed them to accept. Why did she need to press them? Did Paul display some reluctance to accept? It is very possible. He would have no qualms about visiting the home of a Gentile. Why, then, did she need to press them? The clue to his hesitation may be found in something he said to the Corinthians. He wrote: ' . . . I will not be a burden to you, because what I want is not your possessions but you.' (2 Cor. 12:14.) What Paul wanted more than anything else was to see the Corinthians mature in the Christian life, and that was a greater reward for him than any material gifts they might give him. In the same way, he would not trade on the generosity of Lydia, especially as she felt elated by her new-found faith. She could be exploited so easily, and Paul showed a commendable diffidence in taking up her offer. He needed to be pressed. 'And she insisted' that they went.

It seems that Lydia was also willing that her home should become the headquarters of the Christian mission in Philippi and the venue for Christian meetings. When Paul and Silas came out of prison 'they went to Lydia's house, where they met their fellow-Christians, and spoke words of encouragement to them'. (Acts 16:40, NEB.) Today we have our church buildings and we sing fervently that we love the place 'wherein Thy honour dwells'. And yet we are rediscovering the value of the home as a meeting place, the place where informal contacts can be fostered with neighbours and friends, some of whom may never attend a place of worship. Lydia was one of the first to use her home to the glory of God.

In a man's world, Lydia was a successful business woman. She was rich in material things but cherished a deep spirituality. She was on the fringe of Judaism until she became a Christian and a full member of the 'household of faith'. She practised hospitality as a privilege. She was prepared to use her home to further the work of Christ, risking any adverse effect her espousal of the Christian faith might have upon her business in the largely Roman town of Philippi. Lydia set an example to the non-believer in the way she responded to the Gospel. She set an example to the believer in her willingness to use her resources for the work of the Lord.

DEMAS

The deserter

2 TIMOTHY 4:10

Desertion is a word that has a chilling sound to it. It implies the ultimate in humiliation and disgrace. If a soldier abandons his post or absconds from the army, his punishment may well be an ignominious court-martial. In some countries the deserter would face a firing squad. Numbered among the colleagues of Paul was one man of whom the apostle wrote, 'Demas . . . has deserted me.' Unlike John Mark, who made up for his desertion of Paul and Barnabas, there is no evidence to suggest that Demas ever returned to Christian service or rejoined the apostle Paul.

Demas was not the last to desert. There have been many in the history of the Church who have shown great promise and started serving Christ with enthusiasm only to be sidetracked from the path of obedience. From the little we know of Demas, we may learn something about spiritual regression.

DECLINE WAS PROBABLY GRADUAL

William Barclay has drawn our attention to the fact that in the three references to Demas there is a gradual 'cooling off'. In the letter to Philemon (verse 24) Demas is described as a fellowlabourer (Greek: *sunergos*, which literally means 'co-worker'). The word implies that two people are working together as partners, sharing work and responsibility. There is even a suggestion of equality in the word co-worker. Demas was a partner of Paul, sharing the apostle's vision of winning the world for Jesus Christ. That is the first picture we are given of Demas, a partner, a co-worker.

The next reference to Demas occurs in the letter to the Colossians (4:14). Demas is mentioned, but without any accompanying comment, whereas most of the other men named in the Colossian passage are complimented in some way. Was Demas beginning to lose his 'first-love'? Was the vision of life as obedience to God's high calling in Christ beginning to fade? Was Demas drifting from the centre, where the action and the tension made demands upon him, to the more comfortable fringe of things?

The final reference to Demas is the one found in our text where he is described as a deserter who loved this present world. Through these three references, then, we can trace a progressive decline from a fellow-worker to a deserter. Those who fall away from a life of active service rarely do so as the result of a sudden decision; it is much more likely to be the result of an insidious process than a sudden crisis. Attendance at worship becomes spasmodic; the Bible is no longer read regularly, prayer is neglected; there may not even be a conscious decision to desert; it happens by default. C. H. Spurgeon once said, 'Backsliding begins with a dusty Bible.'

Without nourishment for the inner life a kind of spiritual anorexia sets in. When this happens, the prognosis is at best a lukewarm Christianity and at worst, a falling away from the faith altogether.

Concert pianist Paderewski, at the height of his fame, is reputed to have said: 'If I miss practice for one day my professor can tell the difference in my playing; if I miss practice for two days, I can tell the difference; if I miss practice for three days, everyone can tell the difference.' Something like that can happen with regard to our spiritual life: if we miss out on our communion with God, if we neglect fellowship with other Christians in worship, if we get too busy to read the Bible, such neglect will take its toll on our spiritual vitality, and listlessness and indifference can set in.

A LOVE OF THE WORLD

What does Paul mean when he describes Demas as loving the present world? How is he using this word 'world'? He evidently did not believe that there is anything inherently evil about the physical world, since he believed that God created it. In his address on Mars Hill he said that God made the world 'and everything in it' (Acts 17:24). So that when he speaks of the 'world' he is not thinking of mountains and rivers; he is not thinking of the created world. Nor is he thinking of something more abstract such as music or science. There is certainly nothing wrong in loving the world that God has created.

It is clear, then, that Paul is using the word 'world' in a particular way. Just as we might speak of the 'world of music' or the 'world of sport' so Paul is thinking of the 'world of unbelief and rebellion'. By 'world' he means 'humanity in rebellion against God, the world of human reality in so far as it is distinguished by this rebellion and destined for judgement'. We cannot make the simple equation, therefore, that the person who has money or possessions is 'worldly'. Nor is that person worldly who loves life and enjoys the natural world. Whatever encourages ways of thinking and behaving which are opposed to the purpose of God for our lives may be characterized as worldly. Oliver Cromwell, writing to his daughter, offered a definition: 'Worldliness', he wrote, 'is anything which cools your desires after Christ'.

It is not the world itself that constitutes worldliness but how the world is used. A proper concern for money is not worldly but covetousness is; sex within a loving, married relationship is not worldly but promiscuity is; worldliness is life that is lived out of harmony with the good purposes of God.

What form a 'love of the world' took in Demas' case is not recorded. In fact we are not sure in what way Demas was a deserter. There are two possibilities. On the one hand, he may have renounced the faith and returned to a non-Christian way of life; in a word, he may have apostatized and ceased to be a Christian believer. On the other hand, Demas may have simply given up his involvement in the mission plans of the apostle Paul. We notice, for instance, that Paul does not say that Demas has deserted Christ. It is also interesting that Paul knows where Demas is — at Thessalonica. The fact that Paul knew where Demas was living may further support the idea that Demas was still in touch with the Church, although he had abandoned Paul. But even if Demas had retained his link with the church at Thessalonica, it is clear that he had opted for a reduced obedience so as to pursue more mundane things such as wealth, pleasure, and a more settled kind of lifestyle than was possible working with Paul.

Whether Demas actually fell away from the faith then, or simply drifted to the fringe of the Church and opted for a minimal involvement, his example stands as a warning to all Christians. Even an ardent worker can lose his 'first love' and be sidetracked from the high calling in Christ Jesus. What happened to Demas challenges us to look at our discipleship afresh and ask whether we are moving forward and growing in strength and grace and love, or are we going backwards, infatuated with worldly concerns to the exclusion of the spiritual. This seems to be the challenge left with us as we read the sad words written by Paul to Timothy about Demas.

ERASTUS
The VIP at Corinth
ROMANS 16:23b

Among Paul's friends in the church at Corinth was a man who occupied an important post in the City Hall. Erastus had become one of the chief administrators of the city. His office is described by the Greek word *oikonomos*. What was an *oikonomos*? Originally, it was used of a manager who looked after a household or estate. Various words are employed in English translations to convey the meaning of *oikonomos* . . .

Authorized Version — 'the chamberlain of the city'

Revised Standard — 'the treasurer of this city'

J. B. Phillips — 'our town clerk'

New International Version — 'the city's director of public works'.

Certainly, the *oikonomos* supervised the finances, but he was obviously more than a financial secretary carrying out the wishes of a committee. He would have a measure of power and be involved in decision-making in the city. Erastus occupied this important position when Paul was writing his letter to the Romans, and he asked the apostle to include his name in the good wishes which were being sent to the Christians at Rome.

The name Erastus, however, presents us with a biblical teaser: we cannot be sure whether there were one of two of Paul's friends who bore the name. There was an Erastus who accompanied Timothy to Macedonia during Paul's stay at Ephesus (Acts 19:22), and we may assume that this Erastus was one of the typical helpers associated with Paul who engaged in preaching on a kind of roving commission to the churches.

The question we are left to ponder is this: Did the Erastus who worked with Timothy in Macedonia become the chief administrator at Corinth? Opinion is divided on the question. Clearly, there could have been two different men of the same name since the name Erastus was not an uncommon one. There are, however, reasons for believing that we are reading about the same person.

We know that the Erastus of 2 Timothy 4:20 'stayed behind at Corinth'. This means that the Erastus who was with Timothy in Macedonia, as one of Paul's assistants (Acts 19:22), was later staying at Corinth. This could mean that Erastus went on from Macedonia down as far as Corinth and decided to stay there, enjoying a meteoric rise to a position of power in the city. When we remember the cosmopolitan character of the city there seems to be no reason, if Erastus possessed the required ability and expertise, why he should not have risen to high office in Corinth.

From what we know of Erastus in Scripture, he continues to speak to us in at least three specific ways:

A DISCIPLE IN FULL-TIME
SERVICE AND SECULAR PROFESSION

If, as we have surmised, the travelling assistant of Paul did become the city treasurer at Corinth, then we have here an interesting example of how a person who was engaged in Christian service could switch to a secular-political-fiscal post and be a good disciple of Christ by giving conscientious service to the city. This may well mean that in the early Church there was a flexible attitude towards the concept of a Christian vocation. Just as Paul could revert to tentmaking, so Erastus might take up a post in the 'City Hall' at Corinth. He would be no less a servant of Christ working in the office at Corinth than he was while visiting churches with a more 'spiritual' kind of ministry. Sir Frederick Catherwood, a former chairman of the Economic Development Board who became a member of the European Parliament, was convinced, as a young Christian, that he would become a minister or missionary. His father, however, insisted that he should first train to be an accountant and keep his options open. As time went by, Fred Catherwood realized that his gifts fitted him to continue in business and commerce, and that he could best work out the challenge of discipleship in the world of business: thus following the example of Erastus!

The testimony of Cliff Richard furnishes us with another example. He experienced a vivid conversion to Christ and after this experience he automatically assumed the he would have to leave the 'dubious' world of showbiz so as to avoid all its temptations and pitfalls. His mind turned to the possibility of training to be a teacher so that he could teach religious education as the best way of exercising a Christian influence. He believes, however, that just as he was about to burn his boats with showbiz, God showed him that it would be a mistake. He realized, just in time, that the influence his singing had given him could be put to use in terms of a much wider witness for Christ. It was God's will for him to go on singing. Since that time he has had many opportunities to share the story of his own faith with great numbers of people over a period of many years. He has also made many in the Western World aware of the plight of the hungry and deprived in the Third World.

Erastus was the forerunner of Christians who use secular work and the way it is undertaken to become a witness for Jesus Christ. An interesting archaeological find at Corinth suggests that Erastus was very generous and public-spirited in his attitude to the city. An inscription reads: 'Erastus laid this pavement at his own expense, in appreciation of his appointment as aedile.' If this is the same Erastus of Romans chapter sixteen, then it shows that although he was a Christian, committed to working for the Gospel, he considered his appointment to be a great honour. It also shows that he was deeply committed to the city of Corinth. He was not prepared to dismiss the city as irredeemable. Corinth might be a very sinful place, as we are reliably informed it was, notorious for its immorality, but that called for positive involvement and a Christian input, not opting out and abandoning the city to the forces of evil.

This brings us to the second way in which Erastus speaks to us today:

HE WAS NOT DIFFIDENT ABOUT
CONFESSING HIS CHRISTIAN ALLEGIANCE

As he moved in the upper echelons of Corinthian society, he might have been tempted to suppress his Christianity and take a low profile so far as his religion was concerned. His Christianity might have made him suspect with those who followed the traditional Greek religion with its many gods. Many in Corinth would regard Christianity as a splinter group of Judaism. His Christian profession could have become a liability, a millstone around his neck, when it came to making friends and influencing people in the city. Erastus might have been tempted to be careful that his commitment to the Christian community would not create any unnecessary barriers between himself and the people upon whose goodwill and patronage he depended for security in the top job he held.

It is greatly to the credit of Erastus, and a challenge to us as we read about him, that he did not allow personal ambition to prevent him from openly aligning himself with the Christian community. How do we know this? Our text provides the evidence. When Paul wrote to the church at Rome from Corinth, Erastus asked the apostle to include his name in the greetings to the Christians at Rome. The city of Rome was the centre of the Roman world, and Erastus was the kind of Christian who did not mind if the world knew that he was a disciple of Jesus Christ. In spite of his high position in Corinth, he did not keep quiet about his faith or retreat into a secret discipleship.

Henry J. Heinz, well known for his fifty-seven varieties, made a rather remarkable statement in his will. It read: 'I desire to set forth at the beginning of this will, as the most important item in it, a confession of my faith in Jesus Christ as my Saviour. I also desire to bear witness to the fact that during my life, in which were the usual joys and sorrows, I have been wonderfully sustained by my faith.' This statement we might call his 'last will and *testimony*'. Although he had attained wealth and success, he never lost his sense of values and was eager to affirm, in life and death, that faith in Christ was the number one priority in his life. He was in the Erastus tradition.

This leads us into the third statement about this friend of Paul:

ERASTUS USED WEALTH CREATIVELY

It is reasonable to assume that, since he was the city treasurer and had donated a 'pavement' to the city, he was himself a rich man. He would no doubt be aware of the dangers of riches, dangers spelled out by Christ and the apostles. Perhaps he saw it as part of a wise and creative stewardship of his resources to improve the city and demonstrate the willingness of Christians to be good and responsible citizens. Erastus used his money creatively and generously.

Robert Arthington was a rich businessman living in the nineteenth century. His lifestyle, in spite of his wealth, was simple and frugal. He was passionately interested in foreign missions, and in 1877 wrote to the Baptist Missionary Society, offering to fund an expedition to explore the possibility of starting missionary work in the Congo. The offer was accepted and a Christian work was commenced which was to go on growing right up to the present day. God worked through a man's willingness to use his money obediently and creatively.

From the brief references to Erastus in the New Testament, there emerges the picture of a man who was deeply involved in the government of the city, yet maintained a strong commitment to the Christian faith. He did not allow power or riches to corrupt his mind, but kept a Christian perspective in his life and in his work, and in so doing left behind an example to all of us, especially those who occupy positions of authority or power.

TITUS
The good all-rounder
GALATIANS 2:3

The cricketer who is a good fielder, batsman, and bowler we call an all-rounder. He may not be the greatest batsman or quite good enough to open the bowling, but there are times when his versatility proves to be more valuable than the contribution of the one-skill specialist. Titus stands out in the New Testament as a fine all-rounder in terms of his service as a Christian leader.

We know he was a Greek, but no hint is given as to where he was born and bred. If the conjecture that he was the brother of Luke is correct and if, as is supposed by some scholars, Luke was a native of Antioch in Syria, then Titus would presumably also have come from that city. All this, however, is educated guesswork.

We are on much firmer ground when we claim for Titus that he was one of the most tried and trusted of Paul's companions. The apostle says of him, ' . . . my true-born son in the faith which we share . . . .' (Titus 1:4, REB.) This remark of Paul suggests that Titus had been converted through Paul himself. Of the circumstances of that conversion we know nothing. Was he a 'God-fearer' already under the influence of a Jewish synagogue, as were many of Paul's first converts? Or was he converted straight from a completely Gentile background? What we do know is that after he became a Christian he formed a close bond with Paul.

The importance of Titus to the early Church, at least as far as we are able to judge from the references to him in the New Testament, may be expressed in three ways:

THE TRAIL-BLAZER
It seems that Titus was the first Gentile preacher and prominent Christian to appear among the apostles and

Christians at Jerusalem. Undoubtedly, his presence in Jerusalem would serve as a symbol not only of the multi-racial character of the expanding Church but of the way Gentile Christians were beginning to come to prominence as leaders within the Church. Now not everyone in Jerusalem welcomed this population explosion that was bringing so many Gentiles into the Church. In fact, there were Jewish Christians who wanted to keep the Church completely Jewish, not by excluding Gentiles, but by insisting that male converts should be circumcised and in that way become Jewish Christians.

When Titus came with Paul and Barnabas to Jerusalem, these Judaizers, as they were called, became agitated at his presence. In an effort to pacify them, the leaders of the Church suggested that it might be prudent for Titus to be circumcised. Paul would have none if it; and when he stood firm the other apostles backed down. Paul writes of this episode:

'Not even my companion Titus, Greek though he is, was compelled to be circumcised. That course was urged only as a concession to certain sham Christians, intruders who had sneaked in to spy on the liberty we enjoy in the fellowship of Christ Jesus. These men wanted to bring us into bondage, but not for one moment did I yield to their dictation; I was determined that the full truth of the gospel should be maintained for you.' (Gal. 2:3-5, REB.)

It could not have been very comfortable for Titus to find himself at the centre of this dispute. Surrounded by Jewish Christians, he might have been tempted to submit to circumcision so as to safeguard his own position as a Christian leader. Yet to have complied with this request would have undermined the basis of the Gospel, which is the good news of salvation through the grace of God alone.

Somewhere along the line someone would need to stand up against the Judaizers. It fell to Titus to be such a test case and with the powerful help of the apostle Paul he weathered the storm and played his part in the struggle to establish the full Christian status of Gentile converts without circumcision.

According to Paul's vision of the Church, Christians were to be 'all one in Christ Jesus', irrespective of racial origins. Abraham Lincoln once remonstrated with his fellow countrymen for describing themselves by their country of origin such as Italian-Americans or Irish-Americans and so on. If the new nation was to become one under God then he insisted that they would need to perceive themselves as Americans. He objected to what he called 'hyphenated Americans'. There is a lesson for Christians: those who make up the Church of Jesus Christ embrace the New Testament ideal which means regarding themselves as non-hyphenated Christians. 'There is no such thing as Jew and Greek, slave and freeman, male and female; for you are all one person in Christ Jesus.' (Gal. 3:28, REB.) Titus, then, was something of a trailblazer.

THE ADMINISTRATOR

It seems clear from the New Testament that Paul considered Titus to be an able administrator with an aptitude for organization. He sent him to Corinth to arrange the collection for the needy Christians in Judah. Presumably he was the right kind of man to supervise the arrangements efficiently and in a way that would ensure a maximum response from the Corinthians.

Even more suggestive of administrative ability is the fact that Paul asked Titus to stay behind in Crete to 'sort out' the churches on the island. William Barclay translated the relevant words of Paul to Titus thus: 'The reason why I left you in Crete was that any deficiencies in the organization of the church should be rectified, and that you might appoint elders in each city as I instructed you.' (Titus 1:5, Daily Study Bible.)

It seems clear that there were problems in the way the churches were being ordered, and, whatever the nature of the deficiency, the apostle was keen that it should be put right. He believed that everything in the Church should be done decently and in order (1 Cor. 14:40). Titus was the person who possessed the kind of leadership ability and organizational skill to do what needed to be done to put things right in Crete.

Titus' remit included appointing elders to lead the various congregations on the island. There is an interesting pattern here: Paul delegates tasks to Titus, and Titus, in turn, is to delegate leadership to carefully-chosen elders. It has almost become a truism, but is still worth pointing out that the greater part of good leadership is knowing when, and to whom, to delegate tasks and roles. Dwight L. Moody is credited with the saying, 'I would rather set ten men to work than to do the work of ten men.'

The example of Titus reminds us, therefore, of the need for good order in the life of the Church. It is not glorifying God if things are done in a slipshod, haphazard way. It is glorifying to God if in both our work and worship everything we do is done well and efficiently. Even where there is an emphasis upon freedom, which is characteristic of sections of the Church today, there is still need to create a framework of order within which true freedom can flourish without degenerating into anarchy and licence.

THE ADVOCATE

At one point in his ministry, Titus was given a rather ticklish assignment. It came about like this: relations between Paul and the Corinthians were going through a sticky patch, after the apostle had found it necessary to write a strong letter criticizing the leaders for allowing a member of the church to commit a serious moral offence with no clear censure from the church to make the offender aware of the enormity of his sin. Their silence on the question would be seen by non-Christians as the church condoning immorality. The apostle did not mince his words in demanding disciplinary action.

Such a letter Paul had felt compelled to write, and regarded it as a necessary intervention but he was, for all that, anxious to know how the Corinthians would react to his strictures. Would they resent the apostolic reprimand? Would they reject his advice? Would it adversely affect his relationship with them? He awaited their reply with some concern.

Enter Titus. He was not only the courier bearing the letter to the Corinthians, but he acted as Paul's envoy and had the unenviable task of commending and perhaps explaining the letter in this most delicate situation, when hackles were likely to rise. In the event it appears that he proved equal to the challenge. With tact and skill, yet without diluting Paul's rebuke, he reasoned with the Corinthians, no doubt assuring them that Paul genuinely had their highest interests and spiritual welfare at heart in writing as he did.

For their part, the Corinthians were willing to act on the advice of Paul. They took the necessary steps to discipline the offender, and having resolved the problem, sent a reassuring letter back to the apostle. And so it was that Titus had seen the difficulty through to a most satisfactory conclusion. Paul, greatly relieved to learn of their favourable response, appreciated the part played by Titus: 'His heart warms all the more to you as he recalls how ready you all were to do what he asked, meeting him as you did in fear and trembling. How happy I am now to have complete confidence in you!' (2 Cor. 7:15, 16, REB.)

We do not have an account of the proceedings in that critical meeting, but there is no doubt that Titus exercised a calming influence. His example is worth taking to heart. When relations between other people are strained do we, like Titus, help to defuse the potentially-explosive situation? Like Titus are we bridge-builders? Do we encourage those in dispute to keep the lines of communication open? 'Blessed are the peacemakers, for they shall be called the sons of God.' We are all called to be reconcilers, to minimize and, whenever possible, help resolve strife. It is a searching question to put to ourselves when a situation of conflict arises: 'Am I helping or making things worse? Am I lowering the temperature or raising it.' When relationship difficulties occur in the Church or family the Christian will be committed at least to a damage limitation ministry and at best to restoring a true unity.

As we have reflected on the versatile Titus, we have noted that he had the courage to stand for the unity of Jewish and Gentile Christians without distinction. He was a good administrator and could undertake responsibility for a number of churches. He was a sensitive peacemaker and a skilful advocate. The description of him as 'a good all-rounder' seems apt.

ONESIPHORUS

'A breath of fresh air'

2 TIMOTHY 1:16-18

An old legend tells of a time when Satan was going out of business and selling up all the tools of his unwholesome trade. They were set out on display with an appropriate price tag attached to each item. There was pride, greed, lust, hatred, selfishness and so on, the entire collection of the Archtempter's resources with which he spoils human life.

Apart from the rest, there lay a rather harmless-looking tool which, although apparently less lethal than the rest, carried a much higher price. Satan was asked why this innocuous piece of hardware was so highly valued by him. 'Ah,' explained the Devil, 'this particular weapon is extremely useful and I have found it to be effective with almost every human being. Once I have prised open the door of the heart with this weapon then I can work freely inside.' Questioned further, Satan mentioned that the name of this weapon was *discouragement*.

To discourage people is to do the Devil's work for him. On the other hand, to offer encouragement to those around us is to do something that is positive and creative, and may well produce very good results for the Kingdom of God.

One of the lesser-known men of the New Testament has secured a niche in the history of the Church because of the encouragement he gave Paul when the apostle was a prisoner in Rome. This was Onesiphorus. Paul said of him: ' . . . he visited me and encouraged me often. His visits revived me like a breath of fresh air.' (The Living New Testament.) The word which is here translated 'revived' is used in the Greek version of the Old Testament to render a Hebrew word meaning 'to put new life into'. Onesiphorus brought a breath of new life to Paul when he most needed it. That is rather a remarkable thought: the mighty apostle, pioneer missionary, founder of churches and great teacher, needed himself a word of encouragement. No one is above the need for encouragement.

The intriguing question we are left to ponder is this: Just how did Onesiphorus encourage Paul? What did he do or say that proved to be such an inspiration to the apostle? In the absence of more details, we cannot be sure what Onesiphorus actually said, but there are at least three very likely ways in which encouragement would have been needed by Paul and given by Onesiphorus.

The first way Onesiphorus might have been a breath of fresh air to Paul was that:

HE REPORTED
OPTIMISTICALLY ON THE CHURCHES

We can imagine how concerned Paul must have been about the young churches scattered across the then known world. Many of these causes he had helped to plant. Confined now to a building in Rome, Paul was dependent on visitors to bring him news of these churches. Each traveller who came to visit him in prison became for him a source of information. One of these visitors was Onesiphorus. What kind of report did he give? It would no doubt be an honest account of the difficulties and trials the churches were having to face, yet it would be an optimistic one also, telling of the progress and resilience of the churches. It would be such an account that would refresh Paul.

The Church needs men and women who have the spirit and outlook of Onesiphorus, who will remind us of the positive things about the Church. It is so easy to be pessimistic. Yes, of course, we also need to be realistic about the situation and not turn a blind eye to those disturbing statistics which reflect a decline in Church attendance in some Western countries, nor be unaware of the difficulty of witnessing for Christ in a pluralistic and materialistic society. But there is another side to the coin. Reflect on the positive factors: there are still more people in church over the weekend than there are at football matches! People do not go to church today because it gives them status; most worshippers go to church because they *want* to go and feel a *need* to go. The number of Christians throughout the world is increasing dramatically, especially in parts of Asia, South America and Africa. The Church is flourishing in former Communist countries. These are signs of hope and reasons for taking heart.

To be an encourager we need to remember the words of the old song and be prepared to 'accentuate the positive, eliminate the negative' and this, not because we are starry-eyed optimists but because we believe that God is able to do above what we ask or think, even as His power works in us.

The second way in which Onesiphorus might well have encouraged the apostle Paul was this:

HE EMPHASIZED THE POSITIVE
POSSIBILITIES IN THE IMPRISONMENT OF PAUL

Confined in a house-arrest situation in Rome, Paul must have felt a deep sense of frustration. How many churches would have welcomed a visit by the apostle? How many unevangelized areas were waiting to be sown with the seed of the Word of God? What encouragement, then, could Onesiphorus offer the apostle to counteract those feelings of frustration? Well, he must have said something that lifted the spirits of Paul. Using a little imagination we can suggest a reconstruction of what might have been said by Onesiphorus:

'How frustrating this situation must be for you, Paul! Yet it may still turn out for the best. For instance, when you visit a church and speak to the saints, your presence and words are an inspiration. Yet not all that is said will be remembered, but here in prison you are writing letters to various churches and they are kept and consulted again and again. In the long term, these written letters will prove more enduring than the spoken word.

'There is something else I think you should keep in mind,

Paul. The example of your courage gives strength to the entire church.'

Paul's feelings of frustration have, in various ways, been shared by Christians from this day to ours. Many have felt that their circumstances were of a kind to make it difficult for them to exercise any kind of witness or engage in meaningful Christian work for God. It is at that point in our experience that we need an Onesiphorus to come alongside, and point out the possibilities, and encourage us to believe that God can use us where we are: to remind us that every place needs the light shed by a genuine Christian life.

The third way in which Onesiphorus might have encouraged the apostle was this:

HE IDENTIFIED HIMSELF WITH
THE APOSTLE IN HIS IMPRISONMENT

In expressing gratitude for the visit of Onesiphorus, Paul was particularly impressed by the fact that this man was not ashamed of his chains. This rather suggests that Onesiphorus was a person of some social standing, possibly of noble birth, and the kind of person, therefore, whose image could be tarnished if he were to consort with prisoners. If this guess is correct, then Onesiphorus would have had the means to send Paul a substantial gift, with an accompanying message assuring the apostle of prayerful support. This could have been done by the hand of a courier and without Onesiphorus visibly identifying himself with the apostle in what was a prison. But Onesiphorus turns up in person and identifies himself with Paul openly and unashamedly. Paul is impressed, and it means far more to him than if Onesiphorus had sent a gift with good wishes, however lavish that gift might have been.

There is a lesson to learn from Onesiphorus at this point. The best encouragement we can give to others as members together in the life of the Church is to turn up in person and be part of the work of the Kingdom of God ourselves. We can pray for the work others do, and that is very necessary: we can offer financial support, and that is very important also, but the greatest encouragement we can offer is to be involved personally whenever possible and play our part.

Onesiphorus then, appears only briefly on the pages of the New Testament yet no one could wish for a better testimonial than he had from the apostle Paul. At a time when Paul was feeling frustrated and possibly even despondent, Onesiphorus appeared like a breath of fresh air that put new life into Paul. To give encouragement to others may not seem to be a very spectacular kind of ministry, yet who can measure what good is done when we can be to the discouraged or depressed like a breath of fresh air.

ONESIMUS

The runaway slave who came home to God

PHILEMON verses 10b-11

In the Roman world of Jesus' day, slavery was common throughout the Empire. One scholar estimates that the percentage of slaves 'may have reached one-third of the population in Rome and the great metropolitan cities of the east'. (E. A. Judge, *The Illustrated Bible Dictionary*, IVP.) It does not surprise us to learn, therefore, that from the beginning as the Church welcomed converts from all levels of society slaves were included, and although the Church did not campaign to end slavery it became itself an example of a classless society. The New Testament relates the fascinating story of one of these first-century slaves.

THE SLAVE

Onesimus was a slave who lived in the town of Colossae in the home of a Christian called Philemon. Now if Onesimus had been the kind of person who could accept cheerfully and philosophically his lot in life, he might have found reasons enough to be grateful that, at least, he was a slave in the home of a fine Christian. His life could have been so much worse in many another household. His master, a leader among Christians at Colossae, treated his slaves with the humanity and sensitivity Christians were expected to show to fellow human beings. One can imagine his fellow slaves, when they had opportunity to meet and exchange experiences, telling Onesimus to appreciate when he was well off.

But slavery was still slavery, and even in the household of Philemon it involved the indignity of being *owned* by another human being; the slave was the possession of his master, just as a farm animal is owned and controlled by a farmer. Never to be able to choose, or plan, or make decisions without first obtaining permission from his master was a denial, even in those days, of human personality. Freedom is a necessary element in human dignity. This has been clearly demonstrated in the world of our day. People want to be free to run their own nation, even if throwing off the yoke of an occupying power will mean a drop in their standard of living. Freedom is fundamental to human dignity.

So it was that Onesimus wanted freedom above everything else: to him it seemed as precious as life itself. He longed for the day when he would be able to call his life his own. Even the gentler version of slavery as known in Philemon's household became intolerably oppressive to Onesimus as his impatience grew.

Freedom, however, may have many meanings, and its true nature on a personal level is not always understood. All too often, people tend to think of freedom as the removal of external restraints; being free to do what they like without hindrance or restriction. Yet this may be one of the most dangerous fallacies of our age. The removing of restraints often leads not to greater freedom but slavery. Tell a young person that all restrictions on drugs have been lifted and that all moral guidelines for sex have been abandoned. Would that spell freedom? It is more likely to lead to a slavery worse than that endured by Onesimus, as the plight of drug addicts and perverts demonstrates beyond reasonable doubt. The worst kind of slavery is slavery to sin. That is what the Bible says, and experience confirms it. Real freedom consists in the mastery of the sins which enslave us and prevent our growth as authentic people. This spiritual view of freedom was of little concern to Onesimus, whose burning resentment against slavery became an obsession, and his only concern was to escape from it.

THE FUGITIVE

When the opportunity presented itself Onesimus was ready to act decisively. Such evidence as there is suggests that he took money from his master and escaped, making his way to the coast to join a ship, possibly from Smyrna or Ephesus, bound for Rome. What high hopes stirred in his heart on that voyage! He probably reckoned that in the great Imperial city, with its cosmopolitan population, he would be anonymous and safe. Free at last!

Unfortunately, some things are better in anticipation than in reality. For months, perhaps years, freedom had been the focus of all his hopes, the goal of all his planning. Yet when he finally got it, it seems there might well have been a sense of anti-climax. Sometimes people find that freedom is not the be-all and end-all of life; the exciting thing it is blown up to be! Here is a man facing retirement or redundancy. He is told that now he has freedom. But if he has no plan or purpose to fill those years which stretch before him, the word 'freedom' may have a hollow ring to it. He may feel that without a purpose his freedom could simply be another form of bondage. Freedom by itself is not enough.

What good is freedom to anyone who is hungry? What good is freedom to anyone who is lonely? What good is freedom to anyone who is troubled by feelings of guilt? As Onesimus wandered through Rome friendless, hungry, and haunted by guilt and without any real purpose to his life, his freedom mocked him.

We are not told the details of the meeting, but while he was in Rome Onesimus came into contact with the apostle Paul. The apostle was a prisoner in the city; so it is probable that Onesimus went to visit him. He would have known of Paul from the Christian household in Colossae which was the venue for the church in the town. It must have impressed the runaway slave to see that although Paul had lost his freedom he was still remarkably free in mind and spirit, with a passionate sense of purpose. The Christian faith, which was the secret of Paul's indomitable spirit, was meat and drink in Philemon's home, but for one reason or another it had not touched Onesimus. So convinced was he that real life could only be found far away in total freedom that he failed to see what joy, purpose and hope the Gospel had given to the people around him. The secret of true life was near to him, but he was blind to it. Young people sometimes think that true life will only be found away from home in an atmosphere of unrestricted freedom.

Before the Gospel 'registered' with Onesimus, he needed to see it at work in a context other than in the home in which he lived. He seems to have been too familiar with it for it to have had any impact upon him. People in our day have had a similar spiritual journey to that of Onesimus. They have needed to see the Gospel transforming the lives of people in a context other than their family circle before it has impacted upon them. Onesimus had to leave his 'home' and travel as far as Rome, before he realized his own need for the faith. Christian parents should take heart if their influence and encouragement do not bear fruit immediately.

What did becoming a Christian mean to Onesimus? Clearly, his life was changed and his priorities rearranged. Freedom from slavery was no longer seen by him as the only goal worth pursuing. Important to him now was the knowledge that he had been made free from the guilt of past sins. Important to him now was the freedom from futility as he found a new purpose to life in the service of Jesus Christ.

The story of Onesimus is the story of every person; the story of you and me. We have a great Master, the God who made us. The Bible tells us that man imagined that independence was better than obedience and so became a fugitive from God. The Bible uses the word 'lost' to describe his plight. Jesus told three stories to illustrate this lostness: a shepherd lost one sheep and searched in every nook and cranny until it was found; a woman lost a coin out of a set of ten and searched the house until it was found; a farmer lost his son to the far country but scanned the horizon, not resting until his son had returned. In all three stories, Jesus was saying that man is lost, that he needs to be restored to fellowship with God, and that God will seek and find each one of us if, like the Prodigal Son and like Onesimus, we come to the point in our experience when we recognize our need of His grace.

THE CHRISTIAN

At this point the story takes an unexpected turn. The decision is taken that Onesimus should return to Colossae to put things right with his former master, Philemon. Whether this course of action was suggested by Paul or by Onesimus himself there is no way of knowing. In fact, it may puzzle us that the apostle Paul appears to countenance slavery at this point in the story; and puzzle us even more why Onesimus, having taken his freedom and enjoyed it for some time, should now take a step backwards and revert to a life of serving his old master again.

The most likely explanation for Onesimus' desire to return to his former master is that his conscience had been awakened. There were things he needed to put right. To finance his escape it seems that he had stolen money from Philemon. Paul implies this in verse 18 of his letter to Philemon, 'And if he had done you any wrong or is in your debt . . . .' That theft weighed heavily on the conscience of the new Christian. However wrong we may perceive slavery to be in our day, he did legally belong in Philemon's household, and as a Christian he might have felt that he should live according to the law.

Thus in the experience of conversion his moral understanding had been enlightened, and he found himself having to face up to the moral dilemma of his situation. The new freedom he had found in Christ was a freedom to do the right thing, and so he felt impelled to go back to Colossae. An awakened conscience must be one of the most convincing signs of a genuine conversion. Before he had become a Christian, Onesimus' philosophy had been, 'It's right if I can get away with it.' That would not be good enough for him now.

Once Onesimus had decided to return to Colossae, his

problem was how to summon up the courage to face his former master. Paul made it easy for him by promising to write a letter to cover his return. In that very sensitive letter, which appears in the New Testament as the Epistle to Philemon, Paul explains the change that had taken place in the life of Onesimus. He pleads that Philemon should forgive Onesimus and be reconciled to him no longer as a slave but as a brother in Christ.

It made all the difference to have someone as powerful as Paul to speak on his behalf. This picture of Paul's paving the way for his young friend to be smoothly restored to the goodwill of his master and be reinstated in the household in Colossae becomes a parable of the Gospel itself. Just as the young slave needed to be reconciled to his master, so every man and woman needs to be reconciled to God. But how? How can sinful man ever dare to approach a righteous God? He needs a go-between, a mediator to act and speak on his behalf. God Himself has provided such a person in His Son, Jesus Christ. 'There is one mediator between God and man,' says the Bible, 'even the man Christ Jesus.' (1 Tim. 2:5.) Through Christ we are accepted by God, and that not through any merit of our own.

Finally, it is safe to assume that when Onesimus arrived back in Colossae he became a most useful member of Philemon's household. He might still technically be a slave but in reality he had become a Christian brother, and this would make all the difference in the world as to how he thought about himself, with a new sense of personal dignity and worth. As he resumed his place in the household, he might be required to do many of the jobs he did in the old days prior to his conversion but he now carried them out with a very different attitude. He now enjoyed a faith-bonding with the other members of the family; now his service would be done as if he were doing it for the Lord.

Some time ago, a number of young people in a church in the south of England banded together to form a group whose aim was to offer various kinds of voluntary help: painting, gardening, shopping, and so on. They wanted a name by which they might be known. They finally settled on the name Onesimus. They adopted the name of the runaway slave who came home to Colossae, but, more importantly, had come home to God, and in coming home to God was transformed.

ARISTARCHUS

Constant through taunt and tempest

COLOSSIANS 4:10

The spotlight in this study falls on a man called Aristarchus. His name immediately betrays the fact that he was not a 'son of Israel'. He was a Gentile whose hometown was probably Thessalonica, principal town and seaport of Macedonia.

The name Aristarchus is Greek for 'good-ruling' and appears in English as 'aristocrat'. Whether or not he was a nobleman is not known, but his name reminds us that most of Paul's co-workers were converted Gentiles. It is remarkable that although the Christian faith was rooted in Judea, the future growth of the Church depended upon a number of fine Gentile Christians of the calibre of Aristarchus.

Aristarchus exemplifies the fact that Paul was not concerned merely to see Gentiles converted, but regarded every new Christian as a potential missionary. This was part of the genius of the apostle Paul and no small part of his contribution to the early Church: he was continually mobilizing people for mission. He never saw himself as a solo act, an omni-competent pioneer and promoter of the cause. Just as Barnabas had brought Paul into ministry at Antioch, so Paul was ever opening doors of opportunity for others to share in significant ways in the mission of the Church. He was eager to harness the talents of new converts in the service of the Gospel.

When we first hear of Aristarchus, he had probably been a Christian for not more than four years, if we assume that his conversion took place around about the time the Church had been founded in his hometown of Thessalonica. Four years is not really a very long time; he was still a comparative newcomer to the faith. Yet Paul was quite willing to involve him in the work of the Gospel. All training for ministry in the early days of the Church appears to have been, to use the current phrase, 'in-service training'. Theological Colleges, with three-or-four-year courses in Divinity, were still a long way into the future. It was much more like an apprenticeship, learning by doing the job. This does not mean that Paul would thrust a novice into responsibility which was beyond his or her capability. In fact, Paul warned Timothy against putting a recent convert in charge of a church (1 Tim. 3:6). But it does mean that Paul encouraged new converts to think of themselves as involved in the mission of the Church from the moment of their initial commitment to Christ.

Four times in the New Testament Aristarchus gets a mention. In three of these he is in some kind of trouble. He is manhandled by a mob in Ephesus; he is on a voyage which ends in shipwreck; and finally he is in prison with Paul. We look at two of these references.

FACING OPPOSITION

In Ephesus, Christianity came into collision with the idolatrous worship of the goddess Diana. The growing number of Christians posed a threat to the idol-manufacturing industry associated with Diana worship; and the craftsmen feared that if the number of Christians in the city continued to increase a dramatic drop in the sales of idols would inevitably follow. From their point of view Paul simply had to be stopped. Their livelihood was threatened by the Christians. The Christians, in turn, were threatened by powerful vested interests.

The champion of the idol-makers was a man called Demetrius, who could show the most militant shop steward a thing or two when it came to rousing people to action. 'Men,' he said, 'you know that our high standard of living depends on this industry.' He went on to impress upon them that if Christianity were allowed to make progress in the city then even the pre-eminence of Diana would be challenged. His words had their intended effect; incensed by the prospects of losing their livelihood, the craftsmen stirred up the whole city into an uproar. Wise friends prevented Paul from becoming involved and he was kept hidden from the clamouring crowd, but they laid hands on two of the apostle's associates — Gaius and Aristarchus — and bundled them into the amphitheatre.

At this point their lives must have been in mortal danger. It would only take one hothead with a dagger, in that emotionally charged atmosphere, for Artistarchus to have met a bloody and premature death. Aristarchus would have been vividly aware of the danger he faced in that moment and it must have been a truly terrifying experience with the mob calling for action. Fortunately for Gaius and Aristarchus, the town clerk, with a mix of persuasion and dire warnings, restrained the crowd and the two men were released. What courage they needed to stand strong in the moment of acute danger. We should not make the mistake of thinking that these men were without fear. Courage does not mean the absence of fear. Anyone who has no fear does not need courage. Courage is fear that has said its prayers.

Wherever the Church is fulfilling its mission it can never be wholly free from the risk of persecution. It may not always be in the form of physical torture: sometimes it comes in more subtle scorn and ridicule. Jesus warned His disciples that they would meet with opposition even as He did Himself. Sometimes opposition to the Gospel comes from vested interests just as it did at Ephesus. You cannot be the salt of the earth without smarting someone. Those who challenged the slave trade were scorned and pilloried by the slave traders and by those who had grown rich by that diabolical traffic in human beings. Wherever the Christian ethic challenges moral or social evils, it will meet with hostility from those who stand to lose.

FACING A STORM

Aristarchus was with Paul and Luke on the ill-fated voyage which ended with the break-up of the ship in a fierce storm in the Mediterranean. Passenger, prisoners and crew were Scattered on the sea, clinging to planks and broken pieces of ship until they were all finally washed ashore on the island of Malta (Acts 28). As he dragged himself up the beach, wind-swept and sea-soaked, Aristarchus might well have reflected wryly on the fact that being a Christian was no guarantee of exemption from trouble. If he had not realized it already, that storm would have left him in no doubt that believing in God and God's care did not mean that the Almighty went before him smoothing out the rough places, removing every thorn from the path, quelling every storm and quashing all oppo-sition. Christians were as liable to be shipwrecked as non-believers.

There are Christians who are disillusioned when trouble comes their way. They experience a sense of disappointment because they feel that God has let them down. They ask: 'Why does God allow this to happen to me?' The reasoning behind this question is something like this: if we trust in God and do our best to obey and serve Him, then surely we are entitled to expect some divine protection for our lives?

When we look at the experiences of the people of the New Testament, we find that there are times when God does intervene to deliver them from their troubles and sicknesses: yet at other times they are allowed to endure them. There are mysteries in tracing the sovereign ways of God and we are unlikely to unravel some of those mysteries in this life. But, whether we are delivered *from* the ordeals of life or are given the inner resilience to go *through* them, we acknowledge that God is wise and sovereign and we pray for His will to be done in our lives.

Aristarchus stands out as a man who had to face opposition and adversity, but came through it all with a strengthened faith and his resolve to serve God as fervent as ever. He stands out as a man who loved and served God, not only in the good days when the sun shone from a blue sky but also through taunt and tempest.

TROPHIMUS
The Ephesian
ACTS 20:4; 21:17-33; 2 TIMOTHY 4:20

A modern visitor to the site of the ancient city of Ephesus can easily picture what an impressive and beautiful city it must have been with its classical buildings set against a backdrop of steep, green hills. Situated on the coast of what was called Asia Minor (modern south-west Turkey) and lapped then, though not now, by the waters of the Aegean Sea, Ephesus was dominated by the pagan cult of Diana, the many-breasted goddess of Asia Minor. An image of this Diana was believed to have fallen from heaven (Acts 19:35) and the people of Ephesus proudly claimed it to be the destiny and high privilege of their city to serve as guardian of the image. A massive temple was built in honour of Diana.

It was in this city that Trophimus grew up and it is likely that it was in this, his native city, where he came to faith in Jesus Christ. From the few references to Trophimus we have in the New Testament it is not possible to draw a detailed portrait of the man. Nevertheless, from several glimpses given in the New Testament, and taking account of the circumstances we know he had to face, we can reach certain conclusions about Trophimus. These may be expressed in four phrases:

THE COURAGE TO CHANGE

Before committing himself as a Christian, Trophimus would have needed to weigh carefully the implications and possible consequences of such a conversion: it was not a step he could take lightly. If his family were steeped in Diana worship, as most indigenous Ephesian families were, his conversion to Christ would have plunged him into conflict with his family and also with the compatriots with whom he had grown up. If we imagine an Anglican living in Canterbury converting to Islam or a Muslim living in Mecca becoming a proselyte to Judaism, then we have some measure of the kind of antagonism that would be triggered by Trophimus' converting to Christ in the city of Diana. At best he could expect to be shunned; at worse pilloried and persecuted. Aware of the inevitable consequences of his decision, Trophimus nevertheless became a committed Christian in Ephesus. Like the apostle Paul, he was willing to risk losing so much that he might gain Christ.

Nearly twenty centuries later, a teenage boy became a Christian in Japan. He was all too aware of the opposition his decision would provoke. For a time he played safe and kept his Christian commitment a carefully guarded secret. He would say his prayers under the bedclothes in the dormitory of the residential school where he was a pupil. It did not take him long, however, to realize that a clandestine Christian is a disloyal Christian. Toyohiko Kagawa decided to confess Christ openly in baptism. He went on to become one of the great saints of the twentieth century. He had in common with Trophimus the willingness to risk all for Christ.

Trophimus in Ephesus and Kagawa in Tokyo faced persecution because they were changing allegiance, but all Christians have to face some form of opposition as Jesus forewarned His disciples. D. L. Moody once said, 'A man cannot live for God in any age or country without attracting enemies.' To be forewarned is to be forearmed! Opposition and persecution, though difficult to bear, can be character-building; they can develop the muscles of the soul. 'If what you are doing is worthwhile,' wrote Hugh Redwood, 'you will be able to build from the very bricks which opposition throws.'

The second phrase which may aptly be applied to Trophimus is this:

PLAYING SECOND FIDDLE WELL

Wherever Trophimus is mentioned in the New Testament, he is always linked with the apostle Paul. We first hear of him after the Ephesian riot when he accompanies Paul as one of seven representatives of the Asia Minor churches taking money to the famine-stricken Christians in Judea. In every reference to Trophimus Paul is somewhere in the frame. From what we know of him, therefore, we could describe Trophimus as a satellite of Paul. Of the team of helpers who surrounded the apostle, no one appears to have been so content to fill a supporting role as was Trophimus.

Unlike some of the other colleagues of Paul, Trophimus does not appear to have been assigned some individual task. We recall how Timothy was told to stay in Ephesus and exercise pastoral oversight of the church (1 Tim. 1:3). We may also recall how Titus was told to remain in Crete to organize a proper eldership in every town (Titus 1:5). Some Christian workers are gifted to undertake a role requiring individual initiative with marked leadership qualities while others are better playing a supporting role. Trophimus might well have been such a helper to Paul.

We ought never to underestimate the importance of those who play a supporting function in the life of the Church. In the first Corinthian epistle one of God's gifts to the Church is described as 'helps' (1 Cor. 12:28). God gives to the Church people whose forte is to be a helper. What does Paul mean by the word 'help'? Some take it to mean a general helpfulness towards other people, but that is something every Christian is called to do, irrespective of his gifts or talents. In what sense could a person be a 'help' in terms of a special talent? One way to understand the word 'help' is to regard it as descriptive of the person who can so complement the abilities of another individual as to enable him or her to be effective in the use of his or her gifts in the life of the church. An example of such a 'help' would be Silas, who served as an amanuensis for the apostle Peter.

A 'help', therefore, may not be a leader, a church-planter, a pioneer, a great possibility-thinker; yet the assistance given by a 'help' may be crucially needed by those who are gifted to exercise leadership. Paul was a man with a vision of the world won for God but Paul needed others such as Trophimus to help him, and he would have been the first to admit his dependence on such help. Every enterprise needs helpers and there are times when their contribution is critical. C. H. Spurgeon emphasized the importance of 'helps' when he quoted the lines:

'It takes more skill than I can tell
to play the second fiddle well.'

An orchestra needs its second fiddles; and not just to make up the numbers, either!

The third phrase we may borrow to describe Trophimus is this:

FACING 'THE SLINGS AND ARROWS'

When Trophimus visited Jerusalem with Paul, some Diasporan Jews spotted him in the city and they recognized that he was a Gentile. These same Jews had seen Paul in the Temple some days earlier. Mistakenly or mischievously they put two and two together and concluded that Trophimus had been with Paul all the time, even when he had been in the Temple, and since most of the Temple was out of bounds to Gentiles, they charged Paul with profaning its sanctity.

It is interesting to note that they did not attempt to detain Trophimus himself. It was obviously Paul they had in their sights, and it was the apostle they were 'gunning' for. This is somewhat reminiscent of how Jesus was indicted on a trumped-up charge. They seized Paul and would have killed him had not the Roman commander intervened and taken him into protective custody (Acts 21:27 *et seq*).

Thus it was that Trophimus had unwittingly become the cause of Paul's imprisonment. He must have felt deeply grieved, frustrated, and possibly angry at the way things had turned out when he had only been doing his best to do God's will. He had come to Jerusalem on an errand of mercy, bearing the gifts which the Gentile churches had sent to meet the needs of the Jewish Christians in Judea. Yet he was beset with hostility and falsely accused of infringing the Temple regulations. Jerusalem, the cradle of Christianity, ought to have been the most awesome place he had ever visited. Instead, Paul was in chains on his account, and he himself was *persona non grata* in a city where Christians were as fiercely opposed as they were in his own native Ephesus.

Trophimus' experience in Jerusalem is an example of how doing God's will can actually land a person in trouble. John the Baptist had discovered that fact long before Trophimus had. John found himself in prison and facing the wrath of a king for speaking God's truth. And long after Trophimus' day, John Chrysostom, Bishop of Constantinople, also found that doing God's will was a hazardous business. He attempted to purge both Church and city, and even criticized the Empress Eudoxia. For his uncompromising fidelity to truth and righteousness he was deposed and banished to Armenia.

Those who face difficulties and opposition as Trophimus did, for doing what they believe to be God's will, should take encouragement from the words of Peter, ' . . . if you suffer as a Christian, do not be ashamed, but praise God that you bear that name.' (1 Peter 4:16.)

The final phrase we can apply to Trophimus is borrowed from the marriage service:

IN SICKNESS AND IN HEALTH

We turn to the second epistle to Timothy for this final reference to Trophimus. In a brief comment Paul says, ' . . . and I left Trophimus sick in Miletus.' (2 Tim. 4:20b.) With the emphasis upon the ministry of healing in the Church today it is a natural question to ask why Paul did not pray the prayer of faith and heal him. It is a reasonable question to raise when we recall the kinds of things that are reported of Paul in the New Testament. When he encountered the lame man at Lystra he healed him (Acts 14:8f). Elsewhere in the Acts we read, 'God did extraordinary miracles through Paul.

Handkerchiefs and aprons that had touched him were taken to the sick and their illnesses were cured and the evil spirits left them.' (Acts 19:11, 12.) Then there was the case of the young man, Eutychus, who is known for the dubious distinction of falling asleep while Paul was preaching, and tumbling from the third storey of the building at Troas. He was taken for dead, but Paul embraced him and he was restored to life (Acts 20:9, 10). When, then, it seems reasonable to ask, did Paul leave Trophimus sick?

It is clearly a mistake to assume that every illness was summarily healed in the New Testament. In the apostolic age there were people who were healed and there were people who were not. We have noted some of the instances where healing was received. But there were those who were not instantly healed and might not have been in their lifetime. Trophimus was left sick at Miletus. Epaphroditus, the Philippian who spent some time with Paul at Rome, was 'ill and almost died. But God had mercy on him'. (Philippians 2:27.) Epaphroditus must have been ill for some time during his stay with Paul even though he might have recovered in the end because 'God had mercy on him'. Then there was Paul's own 'thorn in the flesh' (2 Cor. 12:7-10) which is generally believed to have been a physical ailment, possibly an eye defect. Timothy was another case. He suffered with stomach trouble and was advised to drink wine instead of water because of his 'frequent illnesses' (1 Tim. 5:23).

There are those in the Church today who contend that every sick believer ought to be healed when the prayer of faith is offered, and the only thing that prevents that prayer from being answered is a lack of faith. This teaching does not square with these examples of illness in the New Testament. Paul nowhere suggests that a defective faith was the reason for the non-healing of Trophimus, Timothy or himself. Healings happened but not everyone was healed. The fact that some were not healed did not cast doubt on the genuineness of the healings that did take place, and the fact that some were healed did not mean that they were more spiritual, or virtuous, or possessed a more advanced kind of faith than those who were not healed. Healing is given as a gift and is not earned or demanded. Michael Baughen comments helpfully, 'God does heal but some are not healed. Factually, most are not, even in the most vigorous healing churches. We pray and seek God's healing; we rejoice when He gives it directly or through medical means; we worship and trust Him when that healing does not come. Prayer for healing in the context of worship and a desire for God's will leaves us with no tensions, no losing of faith and no awkward explanations, or unkind condemnations. Rather it allows us to be centred trustfully and joyfully on the Lord Himself.' Trophimus remained loyal in sickness and in health.

From these few glimpses of Trophimus in the New Testament we are left with the picture of a man who had the courage to change; a man who was willing to play a supporting role with good grace; a man who came through a severe testing; and a man who was required to remain trustful and loyal, even in sickness.

PHOEBE

The patron of many

ROMANS 16:1

In the Gilbert and Sullivan operetta, 'The Yeoman of the Guard', Colonel Fairfax is told that he is soon to meet Phoebe. He retorts in song: 'Who is Phoebe? Who the deuce may she be?' We are setting out to answer a similar question. Who was the New Testament Phoebe?

The text makes it clear that Phoebe was highly commended as a Christian by the apostle Paul. In a kind of testimonial to her he draws attention to the fact that she had carried the responsibility of office in the church at Cenchreae and had been a good friend to many. By paying tribute to her in this way to the Roman Christians, Paul was paving the way for Phoebe to be readily accepted by the church at Rome.

What Paul did for Phoebe is done by some churches today. When a member moves from one town to another, a letter of commendation is sent from the church he or she is leaving behind to the church in which that member intends to settle. Such a letter, which may include references to the personal gifts and talents of the moving member, helps towards a smooth transfer into the new church. In the selfsame way, Paul was eager to ensure a warm welcome for Phoebe when she arrived in the city of Rome, where it appears she was to spend some time.

Phoebe was a citizen of Cenchreae, a small coastal town near Corinth which served as a port for the city. It is likely that the church at Cenchreae was formed as a branch of the Corinthian church, and might have been planted by Paul during his extended stay at Corinth (Acts 18:18). In fact it is possible that Paul might have been given hospitality at Phoebe's home while he was pioneering in Cenchreae, since he can say of her, 'for she has been a great help to many people, including me.' There is an interesting suggestion that

Phoebe was the courier who carried the letter of Paul to the Romans, but the only reason for this supposition appears to be that her name appears first in the list given in the sixteenth chapter of Romans. What, then, can we learn from Phoebe?

SHE WAS KEEN TO LINK UP WITH THE CHURCH IN NEW SURROUNDINGS

It is possible that as she looked forward to a stay in the city of Rome she might have been tempted to think, 'Having carried many responsibilities in the church at Cenchreae, maybe it's time to enjoy the opportunity of seeing the sights of Rome and not become too involved with the church there. I shall be content to attend their meetings as an occasional and semi-anonymous visitor.' If such a thought did cross Phoebe's mind it did not seriously influence her attitude. On the contrary, she had probably expressed to Paul the eagerness with which she looked forward to meeting the Roman Christians, to share with them the mutual encouragement and enrichment that is part of true fellowship in Christ. She was aware that in her new surroundings she would need, more than ever, to be sustained by others who shared the faith.

It is sometimes necessary in our society today for some people to move from one town to another in order to find employment. For Christians, this can mean changing from one church to another and will involve making adjustments and relating to a new set of friends. Some people find this difficult and in some cases, because they fail to settle in a new church, they are lost to the wider Church.

It is not uncommon to hear someone in this situation express his or her misgivings like this: 'I know I shall find it difficult to settle in a church that is unfamiliar to me. I doubt whether any other church could ever mean as much to me as my home church.' Such a strong attachment to one's 'home' church, with its many nostalgic associations, is natural, yet our prior loyalty is to the head of the Church, the Lord Jesus Christ, and, because we belong to Him we are part of His universal Church which is His *body*. It is His will that we should be part of His people wherever we may be and not 'to neglect the assembling of ourselves together' (Heb. 10:25, RAV).

Phoebe is an example to all who have to relocate. In planning what was probably an extended stay in Rome, she made it a priority to seek out the Christians in the city and worship with them. She would gain new insights about the faith from a different church, and she would have much herself to contribute to the Roman church.

SHE IS DESCRIBED AS A 'DEACON'

The Greek word used to explain Phoebe's role in the Cenchreaen church is the word *diakonos*. It may mean 'servant' in the general sense of a worker and supporter of the church. But *diakonos* is also a technical term for someone who has been appointed by the church to serve in an official leadership capacity. Writing to the Philippians, for instance, Paul refers to the 'bishops and deacons' (*diakonoi*). The big question mark that attaches to Phoebe is whether she was a deacon in the sense of an office bearer or simply a notable 'servant' of the church in the sense that all Christians ought to be diligent in the service of their church.

Some expositors have taken the word to mean that Phoebe was nothing more than an exceptionally good member of the church. But this is probably not the best interpretation. It is likely that if she had merely fulfilled some practical role as an ordinary member of the church, Paul would have used the verb 'to serve' or even the noun 'service' to describe what Phoebe did in the church.

From the earliest days the term deacon had been used to designate a believer who had been set apart for an authoritative and leadership role in the church. *Diakonos* in the sense of an office bearer is used in Acts 6:1-6; Philippians 1:1; and 1 Timothy 3:8, 12. When *diakonos* is used in the general sense of 'servant' it is usually linked with God or Christ as in the phrase, a 'servant of God' (Romans 13:4; 2 Cor. 6:4), and the phrase, 'servant of Christ' (Col. 1:7; 1 Tim. 4:6).

We have the weight of probability on our side, therefore, if we regard Phoebe as a deacon at Cenchreae. C. H. Dodd commented, ' . . . we may assume that whatever the deacons were at Philippi that Phoebe was at Cenchreae.' This means that around AD60 one of the churches of the apostolic era had a woman deacon and Paul not only knew about it but raised no difficulty about the church at Cenchreae conferring authority and responsibility upon a woman.

It should be carefully noted also that the word used to describe Phoebe is masculine and should be rendered 'deacon'. To translate it as 'deaconess', as the Revised Standard Version does, is not only incorrect but anachronistic, since it suggests an order of deaconesses which came into being much later. Phoebe was a co-equal of male deacons. What was the ministry of deacons which was shared by Phoebe? One writer observes, 'Since Paul's numerous uses of *diakonos* for himself and the various male co-workers portray them as missionaries entrusted with preaching and ministering within churches, the same must be assumed of Phoebe. She was evidently a teacher and missionary in the church of Cenchreae.' (Florence M. Gillman, *Women Who Knew Paul*, page 63.)

DESCRIBED BY PAUL AS 'OUR SISTER'

She was a Gentile Christian, as her Greek name suggests, but so far as Paul was concerned she was a full member of the Christian family; she was his sister in Christ. There was only one status within the Christian community, that of brothers and sisters, regardless of Jewish or Gentile ethnicity.

Within the Church there were different ministries to which individuals were called — apostles, pastors, elders, and deacons — and great honour was bestowed on those who were chosen to serve God in a particular calling, but this only implied a distinction of function and not of status. Paul was an apostle; Phoebe was a deacon, 'apostle' and 'deacon' were the vocational roles they filled in the life of the Church, but in terms of status they were *brother* and *sister* in the family of God.

The meanings of the names of various leadership roles demonstrate conclusively that they were conceived as 'job descriptions' and not as levels of hierarchical status. Apostle means 'one who is sent'; deacon meant 'one who serves'; pastor meant 'one who shepherds'; and, whereas these roles would involve a degree of authoritative leadership within the life of the Church, they did not create a hierarchy. All Christians enjoy the same status as brothers and sisters in Christ.

When the New Testament speaks of Christians as brothers and sisters, the metaphor implies that they are children in the family of God. Christians have the authority of the New Testament, therefore, to call themselves the children of God. Now to some people it sounds incredibly presumptuous on the part of Christians to describe themselves as children of God in some exclusive way. These objectors would argue that if God created us then we are all, by virtue of being human, the children of God. This belief that God is the Father of all is known as the Universal Fatherhood of God.

Now let this much be readily admitted that God is the Creator of all and He loves the whole world of humanity, irrespective of race or colour. These are two fundamental presuppositions of the Christian faith: God is love: God loves all people. The apostle Paul agreed with the Greek poets that all human beings are 'God's offspring' (Acts 17:28, 29). Yet the human race has become estranged from God, and when the New Testament speaks of the 'children of God' it invariably refers to those who have *become* children of God by accepting Jesus Christ into their lives as Saviour and Lord. John's gospel makes this crystal clear when it says that Jesus was rejected by His own people, but to all who will accept Him and put their trust in Him He gives the right to become the 'children of God' (John 1:12, 13). Becoming a 'child of God' is not, therefore, something a person can merit or earn;

it is the gift of God to those who accept Jesus Christ as Saviour and Lord. And so for those who are saved by the grace of God the claim to be a child of God, far from being a presumptuous boast, is a witness to God's love and the undeserved favour He shows to all who come to Him in repentance and faith.

A 'PATRONESS' OF MANY

In translating this description of Phoebe, the best-known versions of the New Testament avoid the word 'patroness', and substitute some other word such as 'helper' or 'help' and 'friend'. Professor James Dunn has pointed out, however, that the most natural sense of the Greek word, *prostatis*, is 'patron' (see his *Commentary on Romans*, vol. 11, in the Word Series, page 888). If we take the word in its most obvious sense, therefore, it means that Phoebe was a rich and influential person who had acted as a protector and benefactor to many.

We could wish at this point that Paul had given more information as to how Phoebe acted as patron. We can only speculate that it might have meant using her home hospitably, or financially helping people in straitened circumstances, or perhaps sponsoring people in some way. Phoebe's home town of Cenchreae was the seaport of Corinth and was noted for its immorality. There would be many wrecked lives needing someone to care. Did Phoebe assist some of those who were casualties of their own degeneracy? If so, this would have meant that she exercised a caring ministry to those outside the Church. These are guesses and all we can say with certainty is that Phoebe had an outgoing ministry to others which she combined with her role as deacon, and that she used her considerable resources for the good purposes of God in serving others.

So we come to the end of our study of Paul's brief but revealing commendation of Phoebe. We have noted four factors in this commendation: Phoebe was eager to link up with the church when she moved to a new place; as a woman she was something of a pioneer in holding the office of deacon within the church; Paul the Jewish Christian significantly regards Phoebe the Gentile Christian as his 'sister'; and, finally, she was willing to use her own resources to help other people. Who is Phoebe? Who may she be? A notable example to all of us!

EPAPHRODITUS

A fine example

PHILIPPIANS 2:25-30; 4:18

All we know about Epaphroditus is encompassed in six verses in Paul's letter to the Philippians, yet enough is said in those few verses to suggest that he was a fine example of Christian living. He was a member of the church at Philippi and was sent by the church to take a gift to the apostle Paul who was a prisoner in Rome. Epaphroditus stayed at Rome for some time helping Paul, working extremely hard in the service of the Gospel. He became seriously ill, a development which Paul attributed to overwork, and news of his illness reached Philippi causing anxiety to the church. It distressed Epaphroditus that the church was troubled about him and this persuaded Paul to send him back as soon as he was well enough. That, in brief, is the story of Epaphroditus from the Philippian letter.

Paul speaks glowingly of Epaphroditus and uses five descriptive images.

HE IS DEPICTED AS 'MY BROTHER'

The glory and power of the Gospel shines in those two words. It is a kind of miracle that the Gentile Epaphroditus and Paul, the once fiercely conservative Jew, should become brothers. In using the word brother the apostle was not employing a magnanimous euphemism, nor was it merely a polite metaphor. Both Paul and Epaphroditus shared a common dependence on the grace of God, and through that grace they shared a new life in Christ. They had both been born anew by faith into the family of believers. This is why the use of 'brother' to describe their relationship was more than a metaphor. They were brothers because they shared the same life and belonged to the same family.

The sense of deep kinship believers often feel as brothers

and sisters in Christ can create a stronger bond than is sometimes found between natural brothers and sisters. The renowned preacher of a former generation, Dr Joseph Parker, once said, 'We are under the foolish notion that a man is my brother because we are born of the same mother. Nothing of the kind. There may be no greater stranger in the universe than the one born of the same mother. They are brothers who are one in soul, one in conviction.' We may hesitate to agree too readily with that opinion, for the good reason that we would want to affirm the importance of the family. Yet Dr Parker has a point. The words 'brother' and 'sister', when used of those who are truly one in Christ, resonate with a new and unique meaning.

A 'FELLOW-WORKER'

The use of this phrase 'fellow-worker' tells us that when Epaphroditus arrived in Rome he rolled up his sleeves and became fully involved in the work that was going on around Paul. He did not go to Rome merely to hand over the gift from Philippi and then use the opportunity for a holiday, with sightseeing in the famed city. He wanted to be involved with the work Paul was striving to do even in the restricted circumstances of his house arrest.

At this point the example of Epaphroditus becomes a challenge. The harvest is plentiful, but often the labourers are few. Could we be described as 'fellow-workers'? A minister was asked, 'How many ministers do you have in your church?' He answered, 'Over three hundred!' He meant, of course, that every member of the church had a ministry. Was he simply being optimistic or did he have a church of three hundred fellow-workers? In the seventeenth century, a congregational minister, one Joseph Billio, went to Maldon in Essex and became the first congregational minister to work in that area. Life was not easy for him, but it is recorded that Joseph worked hard for his people and served the Lord faithfully. In fact, he worked so enthusiastically that even today we may still hear the saying 'to work like billio'. What a marvellous way to be remembered! That is how Epaphroditus is also remembered in Scripture; he worked hard to the point of exhaustion in the service of the Lord.

A 'FELLOW-SOLDIER'

The apostle Paul did not hesitate to use military metaphors. Much of the time in his post-conversion life he was engaged in battles of various kinds. He spoke about having to contend with the powers of darkness (Eph. 6:12). He had to cope with human opposition which met him at every turn. In Epaphroditus, Paul discovered a fellow-soldier who stood with him in every battle.

What are the distinguishing attributes of a good soldier?

☐ A good soldier is prepared for discipline. There is the discipline of keeping the rules governing his or her life in the army. There is the discipline of training. There is the discipline of learning necessary skills. In fact, there is no point in becoming a soldier if you are not prepared for discipline. George Washington said, 'Discipline is the soul of an army. It makes small numbers formidable; procures success to the weak, and esteem to all.' Now it is no accident that the word disciple and the word discipline are almost identical. They are derived from the same root. Discipleship involves personal discipline but, contrary to popular misconception, discipline is not the enemy of freedom. The better disciplined a football team, the more freedom and fluency in their play; the better disciplined a pianist in practice, the greater virtuosity in the performance. It is no different with discipleship. Paul advised Timothy: 'Keep yourself in training for the practice of religion.' (1 Tim. 4:7, REB.)

☐ A good soldier is ready to face hardship. It seems that Epaphroditus did suffer some kind of stress-related illness as a result of his work with Paul and it might have been the uncomplaining way he bore it that led the apostle to describe him as a 'soldier'. When Garibaldi called for volunteers to join him in a dangerous enterprise, he declared, 'I can offer neither pay, nor quarters, nor provisions. I offer hunger, thirst, forced marches, battles and death.' He might have been somewhat optimistic to expect a response to that kind of appeal but respond they did. When Jesus called men and women into discipleship He laid down that they must be willing to deny themselves and be ready to face opposition and persecution.

□ A good soldier is willing to make sacrifices. Epaphroditus had left behind a settled life with his family in Philippi and probably a higher standard of living. He was thus displaying the qualities of a Christian soldier in his willingness to make sacrifices. That missionary and devotional writer, Amy Carmichael, wrote a prayer for herself which has been preserved for us:

> *'From subtle love of softening things,*
> *From easy choices, weakenings,*
> *(Not thus are spirits fortified,*
> *Not this way went the crucified)*
> *From all that dims Thy Calvary,*
> *O Lamb of God, deliver me.'*

HE IS DESCRIBED AS 'YOUR MESSENGER'

The word Paul uses is the Greek word, *apostolos*, the same word that is used for the apostles, but here used in its common meaning for anyone who is sent as a messenger or envoy, and not in the technical sense of an apostle. Epaphroditus was sent as an envoy on behalf of the Christians in Philippi; so that whatever he gave to Paul and whatever he did for Paul became an expression of the goodwill and affection of all the Philippian Christians. He personified the Philippian church.

Every Christian is an *apostolos*, an ambassador for the Church and a messenger for Christ. That is a great privilege but quite a responsibility as well. An older man with weak eyesight was reading Cowper's hymn which in its fourth verse contains the line, 'Judge not the Lord by feeble sense', but he misread it and it came out instead as, 'Judge not the Lord by feeble saints'. That's a challenging thought! People judging the Lord by feeble saints. A soldier in the Crimean war said to Florence Nightingale, 'You have been like Jesus Christ to me.' The comparison startled her, but the fact remained that the compassion of Florence Nightingale reminded that soldier of the compassion of Christ. She was a true *apostolos*.

A 'MINISTER'

Paul says of Epaphroditus, 'Whom you sent to take care of my need.' The word Paul uses is interesting. It's the Greek word *leitourgos* which in first-century literature 'conveys associations of sacred and solemn work undertaken for religious purposes'. It is from this word that our word liturgy is derived. We think of 'liturgy' as meaning a set pattern of worship, but its deeper meaning is worship offered to God. The service offered to the apostle Paul by Epaphroditus was not only given in the name of the church at Philippi but also a ministry offered as a *leitourgia*, a service to God. All Christian service ought to be a *leitourgia*, a service done in the name of Christ for the glory of God.

Customers in a certain bank were drawn to one particular counter clerk. There was something cheerfully attractive about him and the way he treated customers. One day he dislodged the small plate bearing his name. On the back was inscribed, 'Do it as unto the Lord.' It was only by accident that the customer saw the sign. It was there to remind the clerk himself that his work in the bank was a *leitourgia*, a service to God, a part of his life's worship.

Having given this fivefold tribute to Epaphroditus, Paul then moves on and makes reference to a serious illness which had brought Epaphroditus to the point of death. We are not told the nature of the illness and various guesses have tried to fill the gap in our knowledge. It might have been malaria which was indigenous to Rome. One writer thinks that Epaphroditus had been busy in bringing people to meet the apostle and that he might have been the first to make contact, for instance, with Onesimus, the runaway slave, who was lying low in the slums of Rome. Was it in this area of the city, known for its fetid atmosphere and squalor, where Epaphroditus caught the germ that all but cost him his life? We cannot be sure. In fact, it may be that Epaphroditus might have been simply suffering from physical exhaustion.

It seems that instead of taking time out to try to recover from the condition, Epaphroditus had soldiered on risking his life to carry out his work for Paul and the Gospel. The word 'risked' in the text translates a Greek word meaning 'gambled'. He threw down his life like a gambler's stake. In ancient Alexandria there was a Christian brotherhood guild whose members, during a virulent plague, risked their lives by visiting the sick and burying the dead. They were called *parabaloni*, that is, 'those who exposed themselves to danger' voluntarily and selflessly for others. Paul uses a different form of the same root word in describing Epaphroditus.

It may be that Epaphroditus had been reckless, yet risk is part of discipleship. Riskless Christianity would be a contradiction in terms. A truly Christian life is a life given and risked. The man in the parable who hid his talent in a napkin was, to his own way of thinking, acting responsibly and carefully. His only fault was that he tried to take the risk out of life. He played safe, but by playing safe he lost everything. There is an old saying, 'A ship in harbour is safe, but that is not what ships are built for.' We can retreat into various 'harbours'. Even the Church can become a safe harbour in which we shelter, whereas God has intended that it should be the harbour from which we sail on His errands. There are risks in every area of Christian service whether at home or abroad, whether in evangelism or social caring, but those risks are part of our obedience. The hymn writer has put this same thought into verse:

> 'Father hear the prayer we offer:
> Not for ease that prayer shall be,
> But for strength that we might ever
> Live our lives courageously.'

The illness of Epaphroditus is relevant to the continuing debate about healing in the Church today. The question may be asked, 'When Epaphroditus fell ill why did Paul not promptly pray the prayer of faith and claim healing from God for his stricken colleague?' If anyone deserved healing it was surely this man who had given himself so completely for the work of God. It is inconceivable that Paul would not have prayed for him. Yet his condition continued to deteriorate to the point of death. The fact that Epaphroditus must have been ill for some time shows that even in the Apostolic age healing was not 'on tap', so to speak, to be turned on every time someone was prayed for.

We sometimes make the mistake of thinking that in the Bible everyone was healed summarily and that the prayer of faith for the sick worked automatically in bringing healing. Cases such as Epaphroditus, and Trophimus who was 'left sick' by Paul at Miletus, and even the case of Paul himself with the 'thorn in the flesh', which he had to learn to live with, all demonstrate conclusively that healing was not guaranteed in Apostolic times. There is need among those who emphasize healing to be sensitive towards those who, having been prayed for, may not recover or be healed according to our expectations. Their continuing illness does not mean that their faith is deficient or inferior, nor does it mean that they are less precious in the sight of God than those who may be miraculously healed. Epaphroditus, Trophimus, and Paul were outstanding Christians, yet they were not healed.

In the case of Epaphroditus, however, he does appear eventually to have been healed. Paul puts it like this: 'He almost died. But God had mercy on him.' This clearly implies that God had a hand in his recovery. Had he got better naturally, it is difficult to see why Paul would attribute his recovery to the mercy of God. God intervened to prevent Epaphroditus from dying and restored him to health and strength. This is what Paul's words imply. Their prayers were answered in the end. The use of the word 'mercy' in this explanation of Paul serves to remind us that healing is given by a Sovereign God, as He wills it in His mercy. The prayer of faith for healing is important, but it ought never to be understood as something to be 'claimed' or demanded: it is given in the sovereign mercy of God.

One final question arises from these references to Epaphroditus in this passage, and it's this: Why did Paul consider it necessary to write to the Philippians commending Epaphroditus to them when he was, after all, one of them? Surely, it could be taken for granted that they would give him a royal welcome home and celebrate his return! Why, then, did Paul take the trouble to cover his return with a written commendation?

The answer may be that the Philippians, having deputed Epaphroditus as their representative, might have expected him to stay with Paul for an extended period to help the apostle in their name. When he suddenly appeared again in Philippi, perhaps sooner than some would have expected, questions might have been asked. Paul makes sure, therefore, that the Philippians did not misunderstand the reasons why he had sent Epaphroditus back to them and makes it clear that Epaphroditus was worthy of all honour for the way he had carried out his commission.

So we come to the end of our study of these references to Epaphroditus. He appears briefly on the pages of the New Testament, yet in his wholehearted commitment and sacrificial service he has left behind a very fine example.

EPAPHRAS
A man of many parts
COLOSSIANS 1:7

One of the finest men to work closely with Paul in the cause of the Gospel was Epaphras. Every mention of him in the New Testament carries rich compliments to his character and work. To read again what we are told about him is to learn something of the meaning of true dedication to the service of Christ. Epaphras shone in three roles.

THE PIONEER

He first comes on the scene during Paul's ministry at Ephesus and it is widely believed that during that period Paul suggested to him that he should go into the Lycus valley, some hundred miles away, and work as a pioneer evangelist. Epaphras was himself a native of Colossae (Col. 4:12), one of the three towns of the Lycus valley. He evangelized all three towns, Colossae, Hierapolis, and Laodicea. As a native of the area he was familiar, therefore, with the culture and the mind-set of the people. He could speak to them as one of themselves and not as a *foreigner*. This was probably part of Paul's strategy. It is a strategy embraced by missionary societies today. In the early days of the missionary movement, missionaries were themselves the preachers of the Gospel. That may still happen, but more commonly the emphasis falls on training nationals to proclaim the Gospel in the idiom and accent of the people.

Epaphras heard the call to work among his own people and responded to the call. Under God he achieved notable success in Colossae, Laodicea, and Hierapolis. Our knowledge of the pioneer work of Epaphras is drawn from Paul's words to the Colossians. He says that they had heard about the grace of God from Epaphras (Col. 1:6, 7).

We can imagine Epaphras, therefore, bidding farewell to

the growing community of Christians in Ephesus to make his way inland to preach the Gospel. We can follow him in imagination as he gathered converts together and began forming small churches in the different centres of population. And we can picture him doing all this, so it seems, all on his own; depending only on the help of the Spirit of God. This courageous man of God we can regard as the forerunner of all those who, in the centuries yet to be, would launch out to work, sometimes singlehandedly, in new areas. As Epaphras tackled the Lycus valley, so David Livingstone ventured into Africa, Hudson Taylor into China, William Carey into India, and Dr Wilfred Grenfell trekked two thousand miles of snowy coastline to take the Gospel to the people of Labrador. These were famous missionaries working in far-flung places, but many Christians working in more mundane circumstances have been required to live and witness for Christ where they have been in a minority of one. Epaphras could be considered to be their patron saint.

It is probably a safe guess to say that the hardest part of working alone for Epaphras was that he did not have Paul near at hand. He was possibly a convert of Paul, and from the first days of his conversion had been guided and motivated by the apostle. It is one thing to be enthusiastic when working alongside someone as zealous and knowledgeable as Paul, but not quite so easy when you are on your own. Those who were close to Paul could kindle their zeal from the fire that burned in the heart of the great apostle. The strength we see in Epaphras is that of a man who, moving away from the influence of Paul, remains as strong, remains as fervently committed, is just as prayerful, just as conscientious. He had learned a great deal from the apostle and would still learn more from him in the future, as we shall see, but his spiritual dependence upon Paul was not parasitic. It is clear that Epaphras had cultivated a personal reliance upon God and was able to stand on his own two feet. It is a measure of his maturity that, when necessary, he could be sent to work on his own and be able to rely on his own inner strength, finding for himself resources in God. It is a good thing to depend on one another as the New Testament reminds us in many places, but we can become overdependent. We know a child is growing up when he or she is less dependent upon parents. To borrow the formula found in Ecclesiastes, we may say that there is a time to rely on others, and a time to depend on ourselves; there is a time to learn, and a time to teach; there is a time to receive, and a time to give. Epaphras illustrates this kind of maturity.

THE PARTNER

The next time we hear of Epaphras he is with Paul again and this time they are in prison together in Rome. From what source do we get this information? In the personal letter to Philemon, who lived in Colossae where Epaphras had pioneered the cause, Paul wrote: 'Epaphras, a captive of Christ Jesus like myself, sends you greetings.' (Philem. 23, REB.) How did Epaphras come to be in prison? Had the Romans taken action against him because of his own preaching? This is possible but unlikely at that particular time. The more feasible explanation is that he was one of those friends of Paul who took turns in a spell of voluntary imprisonment to be with the apostle. Aristarchus was another who appears to have done the same thing (Col. 4:10). If this suggestion is correct, then it gives us some idea of the depth of loyalty shown by these men towards Paul. But why should they want to share this experience with the apostle? There are two possible reasons:

☐ Paul needed help. During his Roman imprisonment he enjoyed a measure of freedom. To a certain extent he was able to continue his missionary work but now, instead of his going out to look for people, they had to come to him! The last verse of the Acts of the Apostles describes what the house-arrest type of imprisonment meant for Paul. 'He stayed there two full years at his own expense, with a welcome for all who came to him; he proclaimed the kingdom of God and taught the facts about the Lord Jesus Christ quite openly and without hindrance.' (Acts 28:30, 31, REB.)

A stream of visitors came to see the apostle during his time in Rome; many of them would be fellow-Christians, but also a number of non-Christians came and were taught by Paul. That Onesimus, the runaway slave, was converted through visiting Paul during the time he was in prison is plainly implied in the letter to Philemon. So that although Paul was technically a prisoner under the watchful eye of a Roman soldier he was still able to continue his work. In these circumstances, a person like Epaphras could be extremely helpful to Paul. There were visitors to greet and entertain; there were letters to write and various other things to attend to, some of a practical nature such as preparing the meals. What finer picture of deep personal loyalty could be found than the way these men sacrificed their own freedom, at least for a time, to maximize the effectiveness of Paul in his Apostolic ministry. They counted their own freedom of less importance than the cause of Christ. This example of Epaphras shames our love of the easy path; it judges our seeking for privilege rather than the opportunity to serve. Epaphras was willing to lose his life to find it again in all the rich satisfaction of knowing he was doing God's will.

It is interesting at this point to pause and reflect upon the fact that Paul needed the help of someone like Epaphras. Not even a mighty leader like Paul was omnicompetent. To be effective he needed others to share in the work. It is almost a truism to say that a good leader is one who has the ability to mobilize other people, to delegate responsibility to capable co-workers. One of the temptations facing a leader is to imagine that he or she must plan, initiate and carry out everything that has to be done. Paul was always creating opportunities for his friends to use their gifts. He believed this to be God's policy for the Church. In the fourth chapter of his Ephesian letter, he says that God raises up leaders so that they might train and build up the whole body of Christians for ministry; it is the body of the Church that carries out much of the ministry God intends, both for the good of the Church itself and also for the world (Eph. 4:11, 12). In other words, the Christian ministry of witness and caring belongs to the whole Church, and it is part of the function of pastors and teachers in the Church to encourage and train every member to be involved, so that the many and varied gifts of people, which are all too often the 'frozen assets' of the Church, might be released for the work of God.

Something very interesting emerges at this point in our study. It may be said that by co-operating, Paul and Epaphras achieved maximum effectiveness in the work of the Kingdom. This is often the case for others. We often realize our full potential as we combine and interact with others without rivalry or jealousy. A footballer may have fine individual skills, but it is as he interweaves in patterns of coherent play with the other members of his team that his own talent will flourish. That is no less true of Christian service.

There is something else that challenges us from the voluntary imprisonment of Epaphras. It shows his willingness to adapt himself to doing the will of God without wanting to pick and choose. He was not bothered that it might be demeaning to spend so much time serving a 'prisoner'. He was prepared to be where he could be most useful and to do what was most needed. True obedience says with Isaiah and Epaphras, 'Lord, here am I, send me.'

In stressing that Epaphras was useful to Paul, we must not forget that Epaphras would himself gain by being with Paul.

☐ This gives us the other reason why it was right for him to be there — to learn from the apostle. To be in Rome with Paul was to be in a unique learning situation, enjoying many a personal 'tutorial' at the feet of the leading apologist of the faith. Up to this time Paul had always been a somewhat mercurial figure, moving hither and thither as he carried the torch of the

Christian Gospel on his missionary journeys. It would not have been easy for his friends to 'pin him down' for very long. In any case, they were always liable to be sent off by him on some mission of their own. This enforced stay in one place created an opportunity for long conversations, and Epaphras could profit from Paul's knowledge of the Gospel and its Jewish antecedents.

We do not have the privilege of sitting at an apostle's feet as Epaphras did, yet we have an advantage which Epaphras did not have — all the letters of Paul collected in one neat volume. When we read and inwardly digest the things he wrote to churches or individuals, we may not be with him but we are learning from him just as if he is with us today. And, like Epaphras, we never come to the end of learning. There is a story of a little boy who came home from school after his first day as a pupil. When he was asked whether he had learned anything he replied, 'I did learn some things.' He looked thoughtful and added, 'But I didn't learn everything; they want me to go back tomorrow!' The Christian should always expect to go back to God's Word to learn some more.

We come to the third role fulfilled by Epaphras.

THE PASTOR

With a true shepherd's heart he cared for those he had been instrumental in bringing to faith. Even when in Rome with Paul he is no less concerned for them. We learn about this from a passage in the letter to the Colossians: 'Greetings from Epaphras, servant of Christ, who is one of yourselves. He prays hard for you all the time, that you may stand fast, as mature Christians, fully determined to do the will of God. I can vouch for him, that he works tirelessly for you and the people at Laodicea and Hierapolis.' Col. 4:12, 13, REB.

The distance from Rome to the Lycus valley was quite considerable — a long sea voyage followed by a long haul overland. Yet the concern of Epaphras for his people was undiminished. They might have been out of sight, they were certainly not out of mind. But it is important to note that he did not simply *worry* about his people; he *prayed* for them. Nor did he merely pray in vague generalities; he focused sharply on their spiritual needs. He prayed that they might 'stand fast, as mature Christians', 'determined to do the will of God'. He could have prayed for many other pleasant things such as health, wealth, and happiness. Instead, he prayed for their growth in Christ and that they might do the will of God. He wanted the very best for the Colossians. What is also worth remarking upon is that Paul knew the content of Epaphras' prayer, which suggests that they prayed together, a prayer cell in a prison cell!

Apart from praying for them, in what way could Epaphras work tirelessly for the Colossians while he was so far removed from them? One suggestion is that he might have been raising money in Rome to meet some emergency which was affecting all three churches. It is known that about this time an earthquake caused death and destruction in the area. Epaphras may have pleaded with the Christians in Rome and elsewhere to send help to his people in their plight. If this guess is correct, then it certainly shows that Epaphras, who was primarily concerned in his prayers for their spiritual needs, was also concerned for their material needs. If this picture of Epaphras, soliciting help for his people's needs is correct, then it is reminiscent of the way Jesus ministered to the bodies and souls of His hearers by feeding the hungry, healing the sick and teaching the principles of the Kingdom. This concern for people in the totality of their situation and the variety of their needs continues to be part of the agenda of the Church in the world today. An expression of this responsibility is seen in the varied work of the modern missionary societies in healing, agriculture and education, as well as in the specific work of evangelism.

From what we have been able to gather from the few references to Epaphras, there is much to admire in his faith and work, much to emulate in our own lives from his example.

He might not have been as major a figure as some of the better-known leaders; nevertheless, he shines luminously as a lesser light in the firmament of the New Testament.